Mel Bay's
The Art of the Mountain Banjo

by Art Rosenbaum

A Survey of Traditional Banjo Styles
with Tunings, Playing Tips, & Musical Notes

ONLINE AUDIO

1. Medley— Hell on the Wabash, Seneca Square Dance [1:33]
2. Rise When the Rooster Crows [2:18]
3. Sandy River [1:24]
4. Medley— Spanish Fandango, Don't Let Your Deal Go Down [3:06]
5. Old Joe Clark [2:06]
6. In the Pines [1:54]
7. Arkansas Traveler [1:31]
8. Tennessee Line Hard Times [1:26]
9. Black-Eyed Suzie [1:27]
10. The Green Beds [3:12]
11. John Brown's Dream [1:12]
12. Rocky Island [1:15]
13. Medley— Mississippi Sawyer, Old Molly Hare, Soldier's Joy [2:49]
14. Country Blues [3:45]
15. Cottage in the Grove [1:13]
16. Sweet Nora Lee [1:31]
17. Little Birdie [1:49]
18. Medley— Stony Point, Buck Creek Girls, Harlan County Farewell Tune [2:51]
19. Kicking Mule [2:51]

Charcoal Drawings by Art Rosenbaum
Photographs by Margo Newmark Rosenbaum

IN CONJUNCTION WITH KICKING MULE RECORD CO.

To Access the Online Audio Go To:
www.melbay.com/96711MEB

Visit us on the Web at http://www.melbay.com — E-mail us at email@melbay.com

1 2 3 4 5 6 7 8 9 0

The Art of the Mountain Banjo

Table of Contents

PREFACE TO THE NEW EDITION

I am pleased that Mel Bay/Fantasy Music have seen fit to reissue my two old Kicking Mule LPs on CD along with this accompanying tablature instruction book, first published in 1975. A lot of water has flowed under the bridge since then, and a lot of banjo strings have been broken (and replaced). A new generation of old-time banjo pickers has sprung up, carrying on old traditions or modifying them, or innovating--and interestingly, many of these, unlike the earlier generation of mostly-urban revivalists (of which I am one), are from the old-time banjo's home regions; much has been learned about the African, African American, and minstrel origins of "old-time mountain banjo", and countless new recordings, books, and instruction tapes and videos have been released. Many banjo pickers of the old school, those who learned local styles in family and community, have passed on. Some are still around: a short drive from where I am writing this in Athens, Georgia lives Ed Teague, who still plays his sparkling two-finger style with an active string band; and not too far away lives Edna "Sis" Guest, who has been persuaded to dust off her old banjo and pick the tunes she learned in the family circle early in this now-waning century.

As I say, I'm glad my earlier work still has a place in this mix. Over the years many people have written or told me that they learned something about the technique and aesthetics of old-time banjo picking from the recordings and notations. In *The Art of the Mountain Banjo*, as in my earlier book, *Old-Time Mountain Banjo* (Oak Publications, 1968), I have tried to present a range of old-time styles, rather than to concentrate on down-picking (clawhammer or frailing.) My recordings, like all the Kicking Mule releases, were intended to be listenable as well as instructional. I played everything up to tempo; and although arrangements and settings were made with the learner in mind (variations, playing a given tune in two or more styles), I played the music as I felt it, and transcribed the recordings in TAB later. On listening to the recordings today, I occasionally say to myself, "How could you have done that? (and have to transcribe it as played, rather than the way I would do it now)"; an example is the awkward but doable transition between "Spanish Fandango" and "Don't Let Your Deal Go Down." But this makes my advice all the the more valid: enjoy the recordings, learn what you can, but listen to other recordings and live players, assimilate styles and techniques, and develop a feeling for the music, learning to trust your own choices and musicality.

Being dependent on the recordings, this book is an artifact of its time, but hopefully it is still useful. I have redone and corrected TABS and done a bit of editing, but I have, by and large, left the work in its integrity, rather than to attempt much updating. But old-time banjo enthusiasts can now range through new and reissued recordings, too numerous to list. Be aware of the important work Bob Carlin and Cecelia Conway have done in documenting banjo styles from African American as well as mountain white traditions, and the revealing studies into minstrel and other 19th century banjo traditions by Bob Winans and Clarke Beuhling, among others. You might want to check out a couple of interesting books, Karen Linn's *That Half-Barbaric Twang: The Banjo in American Popular Culture* (University of Illinois Press, 1991) and Cecelia Conway's *African Banjo Echos in Appalachia* (University of Tennessee Press, 1995.)

Thanks to Stefan Grossman and ED Denson for starting the whole Kicking Mule thing, and for their support in getting me into it. Much gratitude goes to my wife, Margo Newmark Rosenbaum, for her good ear, perceptive comments, and beautiful photographs. My appreciation to Phil Tanner, Gid's grandson, for helping me keep my fingers limber by inviting me to pick banjo with today's version of the Skillet Lickers. And the greatest thanks goes to all those men and women back through the generations who made the biting, moody, lonesome, jovial, spirit-lifting, dancing and foot-patting sounds of the old-time mountain (and beyond) banjo.

Art Rosenbaum
Athens, Georgia
1997

Art Rosenbaum

Uncle Dave Macon

INTRODUCTION

A couple of weeks before sitting down to write this I spent some time in an east Kentucky county seeking out old-time 5-string banjo pickers. I was impressed by two things on this short return visit to the mountains: first, the great tenacity of the tradition nearly half a century after the coming of the radio and phonograph to the mountains, there are still musicians to be heared whose artistic styles and attitudes predate mass communications (though these media did produce interesting developments in the music); and second, the fact that even in a small area there can be great diversity of approaches to the music within traditional perimeters. Those of us who have been involved in teaching and helping to proliferate old-time banjo music have occasionally been guilty of over-categorization or over-simplification, e.g., "Kentucky 2-finger picking", or "Virginia clawhammer", definitively described. It should be remembered that there is much room for personal variation even where these categories hold, and beyond them there were and are innumerable "licks", "strokes", and shades of expression contributed by inventive folk musicians.

This book contains tablature transcriptions of all the pieces on my two Kicking Mule records, *The Art of the Mountain Banjo* (KM 103), and *Art Rosenbaum — Five String Banjo* (KM 108). In doing the records and this book, I strove for a very wide range of styles, tunings, and approaches, so that you can hear and try out many of the ways that creative men and women have developed music for the banjo. The book and records can function as a banjo tutor--the material ranges from easy but flavorful tunes and songs that could be tried by a relative beginner ("Sweet Nora Lee", "Smoky Mountain Cass Moore's Tune", "Black-Eyed Susie", "Rocky Island"), through difficult pieces like "Arkansas Traveler". Some, like "Spanish Fandango" and "Sandy River", are close re-playings of specific performances. Some—"Country Blues", "Rise When the Rooster Crows"— are my reworkings of classic recorded performances that will, I hope, provide an approach to the technique and spirit of great old-timers. This hope is tempered by the realization that Dock Boggs and Uncle Dave Macon are ultimately unique and inimitable, but have all the more to offer for this fact. Some, like "Old Joe Clark", are set up to illustrate increasing levels of difficulty and different styles, and would probably never be played exactly as they are on the record by a country or urban picker, who would instead play what suited his/her taste and level of proficiency.

Tablature is a very useful device for learning specific material. There are several books now available with tablature arrangements of mountain banjo music, among them Pete Seeger's *How to Play the Five String Banjo* (Oak), my *Old Time Mountain Banjo* (Oak), Miles Krassen's *Clawhammer Banjo* (Oak), Eric Muller and Barbara Koehler's *Frailing the Banjo* (Mel Bay) and John Burke's *Old Time Fiddle Tunes for Banjo* (Oak). But you should remember traditional music is oral, so listen to recorded examples, and especially to live players when they can be heard. I hope that my recordings and tablatures will help you in making this music your own, and that you will move from them into your own place in the musical continuum.

Joe and Odell Thompson String Band

THE SEQUENCE, AND THE STYLES

Assuming you want to work through most of this material, it can be done by picking style, by tuning, or in a more hit-or-miss manner, whichever suits your experience, inclination, or temperament. I started out with the old "Kicking Mule", a piece which takes a simple melody and song accompaniment through the four main approaches used by folk banjo pickers. First, there is "up-picking", or Pete Seeger's "basic strum", where the index finger picks up on a string, then the hand brushes down, and thumb catches and picks the 5th string. Then some double-thumbing is introduced, where the thumb moves over onto the inside strings. Then comes the second style, two-finger picking, in this case thumb lead double thumbing, a style known in Kentucky and the southern part of the Midwest. Third, there is some three-finger picking, employing the thumb, index and the middle fingers, in this tune freely derived from the minstrel show approach. Finally, the right hand moves into a downward attack in what has variously been called "frailing", "clawhammer", "knocking", "rapping", "overhand", "fram-style", "frailing", "flayin' hand", and many other Appalachian appellations, for which I invented the term DOWN-PICKING in order to avoid ridiculous arguments about where "frailing" leaves off and "clawhammering" begins. Essentially the hand descends in a knocking movement and the back of the fingernails strike either a single note or brush across more strings as the thumb descends to stop against the 5th or another string which is sounded as the hand bounces up to begin the next down-stroke.

"Kicking Mule" can help you get oriented. The next large section is devoted to a development of the downpicking style and its many variations. In general the progression moves from easier to more challenging pieces, and there is a development from one tuning to another.

Note that many of these pieces are breakdowns, tunes intended for dancing. Occasionally these are played on the banjo alone, but the natural complementing instrument, indeed, the instrument that generally carries the melodic lead, is the fiddle, and sessions with a good fiddler will do wonders for your banjo picking. Other instruments that might be added to the fiddle-banjo nucleus are the guitar, harp (harmonica), dulcimer, and mandolin. Some of the breakdowns have verses that can be sung (including some, like "Old Joe Clark" that are given here as instrumentals). Most of the other selections are song and ballad accompaniments, and the banjo is wonderfully adaptable in setting up rhythmic underpinnings to free vocal lines, and in suiting tunings to various modes and scales used in mountain singing. Many of the songs are of the "banjo song" or "rounder song" category; part blues, part narrative, "born", as Bascom Lunsford put it, "out of the hilarity of mountain banjo picking".

After the down-picking section come a few pieces in up-picking and two-finger styles. Beginning players might find these good to start with, and very satisfying. And players who have confined their efforts to downpicking might enjoy the variety and new possibilities that these styles offer.

Finally, there are several pieces in a variety of three-finger styles. The use of a third finger opens a wide range of options, from the simple but compelling song accompaniments in "Country Blues", through the old-fashioned minstrel show-derived syncopation of "Rise When the Rooster Crows", through the pre-bluegrass melodic flow of "Spanish Fandango".

This book, and the recording, is all tunes and song, no exercises. Experienced players will find some of the material easy; novices will need to break some pieces down, and play patterns, measures, passages, as exercises.

Omer Forster

ABOUT THOSE TUNINGS

Don't let the great number of tunings used here, or the greater number used in old-time banjo picking worry you. Once you can get into them, they are more of a help than a hindrance, facilitating the playing of certain tunes by having many of the notes of the tune incorporated into the tuning, and adding a mood or atmosphere not to be otherwise attained.

You may find that you can do well with a few tunings, or you may wish to experiment with many more traditional or new tunings. In the sequence described above, I have tried to cluster related tunings; it helps to understand which tunings are grouped together.

It is also helpful to pluck two strings that are supposed to be an octave apart with thumb and index finger as you tune, until they ring together.

Or, keep this chromatic scale in mind:

C C# D D# E F F# G G# A A# B C

One fret is the equivalent of 1/2 tone, or 1 step on this scale, so go up a string the pitch of which you know to find a note you want.

Recently, in Kentucky, Shorty Reynolds was trying to find the tuning for "Darlin' Corey", but couldn't get it to "ring in my noggin", though his banjo-picking wife, whose name happens to be Corey, patiently told to him to "tune for 'Little Birdie' and run your bass string up". But instead, he dropped the banjo into the lonesome and beautiful "Cuba" tuning. But that's another record.

And remember the late Rufus Crip's dictum:

"That's the main, the <u>main</u> important part about music, get your instrument in the right tune!"

Dock Boggs

EXPLANATION OF

THE TABLATURE

The tunes on this record are transcribed in the tablature system I used in *Old-Time Mountain Banjo* (Oak, 1968).

Briefly, the five horizontal lines stand for the five strings of the banjo, the top line being the 1st string, the bottom the 5th or thumb string:

The tablature is read from left to right, a number on a line indicates a note sounded on that particular string; "O" indicates that the string is sounded open or unfretted, any other number, that the string is stopped at the fret corresponding to the number. Two or more numbers shown vertically indicate that the notes are sounded at the same time. As for rhythm, I assume that we are basically working in a duple rhythm in $\frac{4}{4}$ time: 1　2　3　4 but that most of the banjo stuff divides the beats in half:

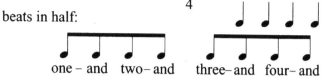

one – and　two– and　three– and　four– and

A single vertical stem below a number, or numbers above one another (a chord), indicates a long, or quarter note:

$\begin{matrix} 3 \\ 1 \end{matrix}$ = ♩　$\begin{matrix} 3 \\ 2 \\ 1 \end{matrix}$ = ♩

Occasionally a long note occurs as a pinch, with the stem between two numbers

$\begin{matrix} 3 \\ 1 \end{matrix}$ = ♩
0
I (index)
T (thumb)

Short, or eighth notes, described above are indicated in TAB by horizontal lines connecting the numbers' stems:

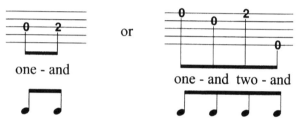

A few signs have been borrowed from conventional music notation:

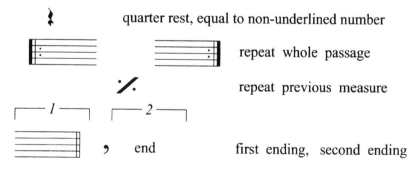

The following signs are also used in the TABs:

→2 　an arrow before a fretted note indicates a sliding attack up to the note from a fret or two below

2
↓　an arrow pointing down means that the note is choked, or pushed to one side as it is sounded, raising the pitch

⌢　an arc indicates that there is some hammering on or pulling off going on with the left hand

0 ⌢ 2　hammer on from open string to 2nd fret

2 ⌢ 0　pull off, from second fret to open string

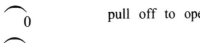0   pull off to open string from unsounded position;

(9)   7   sometimes the unsounded fret from which the sounded note is pulled is indicated by parentheses

Under the TAB lines, and directly under the number-notes, are indications of how they are sounded.

I   the note is picked up, (or, in down-picking, struck downward) by the right index finger

T   thumb picks note down

M   middle finger picks note

B   downward brush by back of nails of right hand

R   roll, similar to brush, but the hand rakes down a bit more slowly, or the fingers are slightly unclenched one by one as they strike the strings

RT   roll, terminated by the thumb catching the 5th string

H   hammer on, by a finger of the left hand

P   pull off, by a finger of the left hand

sl   slide; finger holds string down to fingerboard as it moves from one fret to another

I used several traditional tunings on the record; they are indicated in the notes to the tunes, as well as in the tablature, with the note shown next to the corresponding string.

The picking style is also indicated at the beginning of the tablature as well as in the commentary. I have used the term "down-picking" as a catch-all for the family of styles variously called frailing, clawhammer, knock-down, flyin'hand, knocking, rapping, dropthumb, fram-style, etc.; notes are struck by a downward motion of the right hand, and usually the back of the index fingernail strikes the strings. Downward brushes are also used. The thumb descends with the hand and catches but does not sound the note it is about to pick, whether it be the 5th or one of the inside strings; then the thumb sounds the string as the hand bounces up.

I call up-picking the style where the index lead is picked up. Two-finger picking utilizes right thumb and index finger; three-finger picking uses the thumb, index, and middle fingers.

Here is a walk-through of a typical passage, notated in TAB:

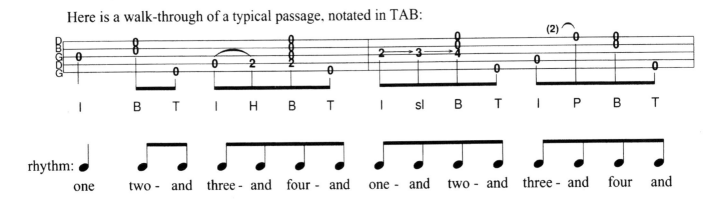

The banjo is tuned in open G : 5th high G

4th	D
3rd	G
2nd	B
1st	D

In the first measure, the right index finger (1) sounds the open 3rd string (picks up in up-picking, strikes, down in down-picking.) Then the back of the nails brush (B) down across the 1st and 2nd strings together. Then the thumb (T) sounds the 5th string (it has come to rest on the string as the hand descended in the brush). Then the index sounds the open 4th string; next a convenient (in this case, let's use the 2nd) finger of the left hand hammers down on the 4th string behind the 2nd fret, sounding it. Finally the right hand brushes again over the strings, sounding the open 1st, 2nd, and 3rd strings, and the 4th, now stopped at the 2nd fret, followed by the thumb, sounding the open 5th string.

In the second measure, the index sounds the 3rd string, 2nd fret. Smoothly, without releasing pressure, the 2nd finger of the left hand slides (sl) up to the 3rd fret of the 3rd string, then continues to the 4th as the right hand brushes down over 1st (open), 2nd (open), 3rd (at 4); Then the thumb sounds the 5th string. Next the index picks (or strikes) the open 4th string. Then the left second finger pulls off from the unsounded 2nd fret of the 1st string, playing the 1st string open. Finally, a brush over the first two strings open, followed by thumb on open 5th.

Note on guitar accompaniments:

Chords are sometimes indicated above the TAB lines. Although some old-time banjo tunes are apropriately harmonized with tonic, dominant, and sub-dominant chords (for example, "Black-Eyed Susie," with C, G, and F chords), many simply work around one chord ("Smoky Mountain Cass Moore's Tune," "Rocky Island," or "Sweet Nora Lee"), and the guitar will have to plunk along, or play runs or double on the melody to stay in keeping with the simple nature of the tunes. Others are highly modal in flavor and usually sound best with just banjo, banjo and voice, or occasionally banjo and fiddle: "Had a Little Fight in Mexico," "Sandy River," "Cottage in the Grove," " The Green Beds, " and "Texas Rangers" are modal tunes where the full forms of the basic chords would not be suitable and if the guitar is used it should play runs or some melody parallel to the banjo. Parentheses indicate a chord the guitar would play, but which is not fully formed on the banjo.

W. Guy Bruce, Trion, GA, with cousin Jim Bruce "beating straws", c. 1919 — *Photo: Mr. Sullivan*

KICKING MULE

ED Denson tells me that this record company was named after a stamp cancelling machine in the form of old time America's most loved but most vexatious working animal, but no matter. I had to do this great old song, sung and played in countless ways by black and white singers. These verses come from the King family's Library of Congress recording and from Smoky Mountain Cass Moore. I use the rather simple melody to demonstrate the four principal right hand techniques employed by old time banjo pickers.

TUNING: G_{CGBD}   This is the so-called "standard" C tuning, the notes corresponding to the strings you buy and to the notes on a banjo pitch pipe; it is not, however, the most common in folk usage. If you have to tune the banjo to itself, start with the 4th string to C or an approximation (medium low) thereof, then tune the 3rd to the 4th stopped at the 7th fret, the 2nd to the 3rd stopped at the 4th fret, and 1st to the 2nd stopped at the 3rd fret, and the 5th, or thumb string to the 1st stopped at the 5th fret.

PICKING: You work from these two chords, the tonic and dominant in the key of C:
(Other songs and tunes in this tuning might use the sub-dominant:

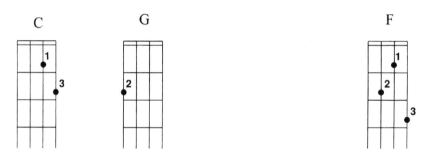

This piece is a walk-through of the four principal ways the banjo is played traditionally:

a) Up-picking, where the index finger picks up on a string, followed by a downward brush of the nails of the right hand across the strings, then concluded by the thumb picking the 5th string, to a BUMP dit-ty, ♩ ♫, rhythm. This is Pete Seeger's "basic strum". Also used are left-hand pull-offs, slides up the fingerboard, and double thumbing, where the thumb follows the lead note by picking a single inside string, then the index picks the 1st string, finally the thumb sounds the 5th string.

b) Thumb-lead two-finger picking, using the thumb and index finger in various combinations. The thumb plays the principal beats, the index the secondary ones, and the thumb hits most of the melody notes. Occasionally the thumb and index pinch the 1st and 5th strings together for syncopation. Left hand hammer-on notes are used in this section as well.

c) This is a rudimentary 3-finger style, using the thumb, middle and index fingers. The triplets call for three notes to be played in the time of one quarter note:

$$\overset{3}{\frown}_{0\ 1\ 2} = \underline{0}$$

d) The down-picking section: all notes are hit with a downward motion of the hand, the lead notes struck by the back of the index finger, the brushes at the back of the left hand finger nails, the thumb notes on the 5th string and the so-called "drop-thumb" notes where the thumb hits the second or less frequently another inside string. This style will be dealt with in detail in the tunes to follow.

Kicking Mule

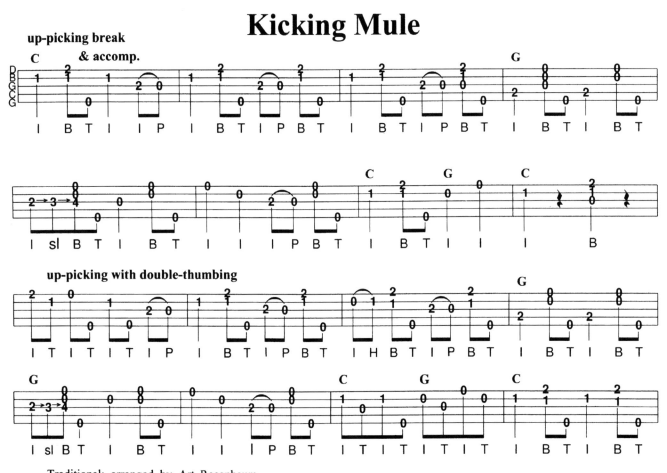

Traditional; arranged by Art Rosenbaum

2- Finger break accomp.

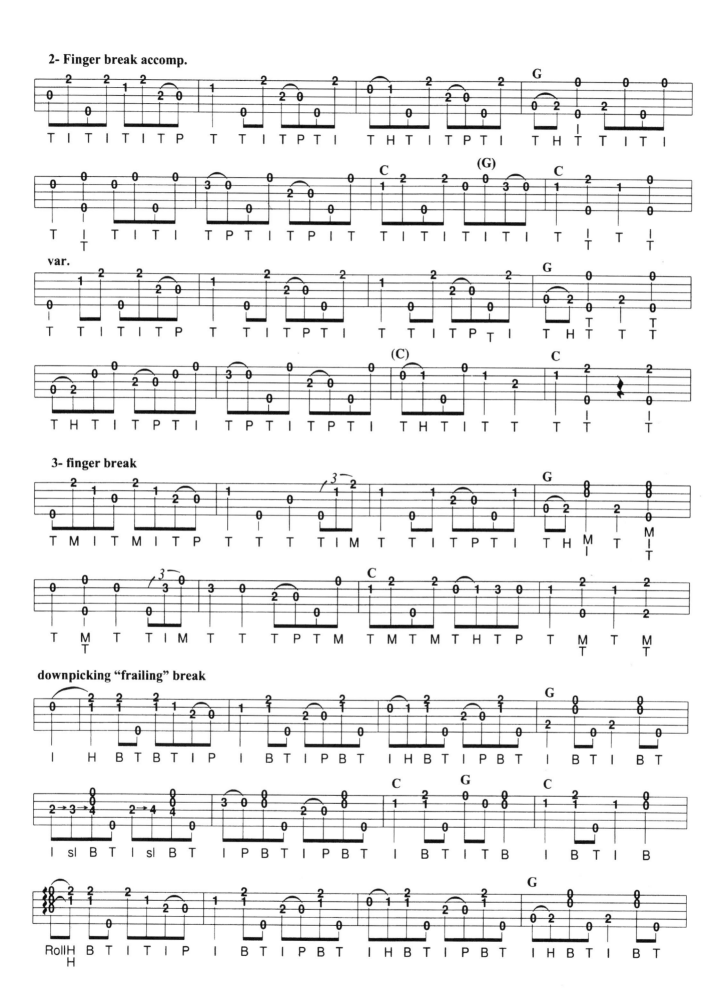

var.

3- finger break

downpicking "frailing" break

Kicking Mule (cont.)

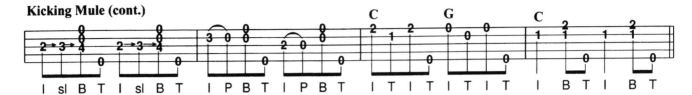

1) I went down to the huckleberry picnic
   dinner all over the ground,
   skippers in the meat were nine foot deep
   and the green flies walkin' all around.

   Biscuits in the oven was a-bakin'
   was a beefsteak fryin' in the pan,
   pretty girl settin' in the parlor
   Lord God Amighty what a hand I stand!

   Chorus: Whoa, mule, I tell you,
   Miss Liza, you keep cool.
   Ain't got time to kiss you now
   I'm busy with the mule.

2) My uncle had an old grey mule,
   his name was Simon Slick.
   "Bove anything I ever did see was
   how that mule could kick.

   Went to feed that mule this mornin',
   He met me at the door with a smile.
   Backed one ear and winked one eye and
   kicked me half a mile.

   Chorus: Whoa, mule, I tell you,
   whoa, mule I say,
   keep your seat Miss Liza Jane, and
   hold on to the sleigh.

3) This mule is a kicker,
   he has an iron back,
   spotted him a Texas railroad train and
   kicked it off the track.

   This mule is a kicker,
   he has an iron jaw,
   he's the very best thing to have around to
   tame your mother-in-law.

   Chorus: Whoa, mule, I tell you,
   whoa, mule, I say,
   ain't got time to kiss you now
   this mule's runnin' away.

4) He kicked the feathers off a goose
   he pulverized a hog,
   kicked up three dead roustabouts and
   swatted him a yeller dog.

   Went to Miss Dinah this mornin'
   she was bendin' all over the tub,
   the more I asked her to marry me
   the harder she would rub.

   Chorus: Whoa, mule, I tell you,
   Miss Liza you keep cool,
   ain't got time to kiss you now
   I'm busy with that mule.

5) See that mule a-comin',
   he's comin' down the road.
   You can tell by the wiggle of his ears
   he ain't got half a load.

   See that mule a-goin'
   he's goin' down the track,
   you can tell by the wiggle of his tail
   he ain't comin' back!

   Chorus: Whoa, mule, I tell you,
   whoa, mule, I say.
   Ain't got time to kiss you now,
   that mule's runnin' away!

DOWN-PICKING PIECES

Ross Brown, Lawrence Eller, Art Rosenbaum

ROCKY ISLAND

This tune runs a close second to 'Hook and Line' as one of the first tunes that Kentucky banjo pickers of the last generation learned. It is good for relatively inexperienced pickers, as the 2nd string is tuned an octave higher than the 4th, permitting easy noting up the 1st string; moreover, no drop thumb is employed... the thumb keeps hitting the 5th string, at times on every off beat. I learned this version from Omie Rose, a coal miner's wife in Helton, Kentucky, on the Harlem Leslie County Line. I had picked up a young hitchhiker and asked him where in the area I might hear old time banjo picking and singing. "Stop at any house on this road," was his matter-of-fact reply. I wanted to narrow things down a bit, and he directed me to Omie Rose's house, where I met a gracious woman who had a powerful mountain voice and a hell-for-leather banjo style.

TUNING: GCGCD   or the "two-C" tuning. From the standard C tuning, raise the 2nd string 1/2 tone, or one fret, to sound an octave higher than the 4th string, or tune to the 3rd string stopped at the 5th fret. The 1st string stopped, or "noted" at the 2nd fret produces a C chord. This tuning permits easy movement around the fingerboard for tunes not requiring full chords.

17

PICKING:

Down-picking, my general term for the downward attack of the right hand sometimes called "frailing", "clawhammer", "knocking", "rapping" etc.. With the wrist slightly flexed, the hand moves down across the string, either brushing several strings with the back of the nails, or striking one or two strings with the nail of the index finger. The thumb moves down with the hand, coming to rest on the 5th string, which is sounded as the hand rebounds to be in position to descend again. Often the 5th string is not sounded after the 1 and 3 beats of a 1 2 3 4 measure, but you might practice a measure like the 21st if you are inexperience in this style and want to get the brush and the thumb working together (Later, the thumb will descend to an inside string, the "drop thumb" lick). The second half of the 10th measure uses a common Kentucky lick where a note is pulled off, then replaced in time for the brush; this works well behind the voice in song accompanyment. Don't worry about precision in striking single notes in this dance tune-- a good solid brushy rhythm is important here.

Rocky Island

down-picking

goin'to Rock–y Is – land

goin'to Rock–y Hill   goin'to Rock–y Is – land to

get my bot – tle filled!

Traditional; arranged by Art Rosenbaum

Copyright © 1975 Kicking Mule Publishing

18

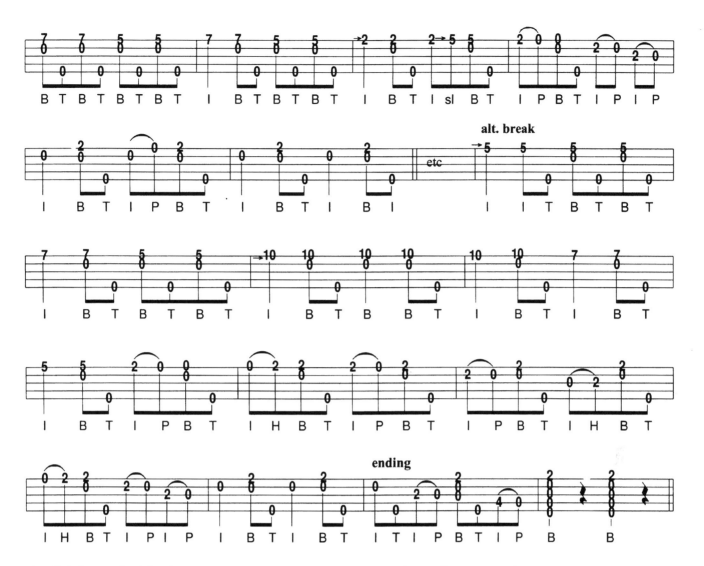

1) Goin' to rocky island
goin' to rocky hill,
goin' to rocky island
to get my bottle filled.

2) See the train a-comin'
comin' down the track
carrying away my true love,
never gonna bring her back.

3) It's oh goodbye my mother,
oh goodbye, I say,
oh goodbye my mother,
I'm going away.

4) Goin' to rocky island
goin' to rocky shore,
goin' to rocky island,
ho, honey ho.

DRY AND DUSTY

Partly the real "Dry and Dusty", partly Illinois fiddler Stella Elam's "Jaybird".

TUNING: ADADE   This is the two-C tuning with all the strings tuned up to a whole tone (two frets) to play in the key of D, a common key when playing with a fiddle. Traditional musicians generally tune up in this manner, but you might prefer to keep the banjo in the 2-C tuning and use a capo at the 2nd fret, tuning the 5th string up one tone.

PICKING: Down-picking. The same attack as the preceding tune, but a more syncopated approach, stressing single melody notes. Some of these are
produced by pulls and hammers, occasionally on the principal accents,
some (measures 10 and 12) with the thumb picking melody notes on the
5th string. In measure 8 this F formation (in this case a G chord) occurs:

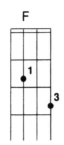

Dry and Dusty

down-picking

or GCGCD, capo'd at 2nd fret, 5th string tuned to A

Traditional; arranged by Art Rosenbaum
Copyright © 1975 Kicking Mule Publishing

LIBERTY

This tune seems to have been most common in Virginia but now is played by fiddlers across
the country. Here, I tune the banjo GCGCD and pick it in a claw-hammer arrangement that
was probably influenced by John Burke's playing.

TUNING: ADADE   or, two-C tuning capo'd up a whole tone, as in DRY AND DUSTY.

PICKING: Down-picking. This approach is often called "clawhammer", with relatively little brushing of chords, and an emphasis on filling out the melody of a fiddle tune, but not at the expense of the rhythm that the banjo must provide. The last measure of the first line introduces the drop thumb, first a full sequence, where the index hits a note (as it does, the thumb drops to rest on the 2nd string), then the thumb sounds the 2nd string, then the index hits 1st string again (the thumb drops to rest on the 5th string), and finally the thumb sounds the 5th string; then there is a half sequence, as the second index note is held a whole beat. Note the 7th and 12th measures, the first string is touched but not sounded at third fret, then pulled, to sound the string stopped at the 2nd fret.

Liberty

down-picking

"2c" tuning (GCGCD) capo'd or tuned up 1 tone, 5th string tuned to A

Traditional arranged by Art Rosenbaum

Copyright © 1975 Kicking Mule Publishing

GREY EAGLE

I learned this from Pete Steele, the great Kentucky banjo picker, who had played it with his father, a fiddler. Kentucky banjo players seldom attempt to work in all the notes of a fiddle tune into their banjo settings, as the Virginia clawhammer pickers do. Their renditions tend to be more percussive and less evocative of the fiddle original. Pete Seeger had visited Pete Steele shortly before Ed Kahn and I did in 1956. Steele had enjoyed meeting Seeger .. "That boy had the interest and he had the music!" He wanted us to play his recording of "Grey Eagle" for Pete Seeger. "Tell that boy you note the thumb string on that." And indeed it is unusual in old-time banjo picking for the fifth or drone string to be fretted, as it is here.

TUNING: GDGBD   Open G tuning. From the standard C tuning, raise the 4th string a whole tone, from C to D (an octave down from the 1st string. This is one of the most commonly used tunings, permitting chord work of single noting.

PICKING: Down-picking. The rolls are downward raking brushes of the backs of the nails, terminated by the thumb picking the 5th string; here the 5th string is noted at the 9th, then the 7th frets, then is sounded open in the third roll. Note the choked notes in the next to last measure, where the fretted string is pushed to one side as it is sounded. The first two rolls are not cut off, but are held during the quarter rests.

Grey Eagle

by Pete Steele
Copyright © 1975 Pete Steele

OLD JOE CLARK

This is one of the oldest and best American dance tunes. I play it four times around, picking each of the two parts twice (when it is done as a song, each part is usually played once, verse and chorus fashion). It starts out pretty simply, with hammers and pulls and a bit of rhythmic drop thumb. The second go round adds some variations and some melodic drop thumb work. The third repeat is based on Wade Ward's unique treatment, with syncopated slides and judiciously chosen notes (hear his original recording on Library of Congress 12.) Finally, a more modern treatment, with passages of "chromatic" clawhammer, where all the notes a fiddler might play are played, and some of the rhythmic under pinning of the older styles is sacrificed to get in more melody notes. A learning banjo player should work through all this and select out what fits his/her capacity and musical sensibility.

TUNING: ^{A}EAC♯E This is the open G tuning tuned up 1 tone (2 frets) to produce an open A chord (the key in which this is usually played on the fiddle.) Or, use the capo at the 2nd fret and tune up the 5th string a whole tone to A.

PICKING: Down-picking. The melodic material of this two-part tune is, line-by-line, basically:

Pt. I	A
	B
	A
	C
Pt. II	D
	E
	D
	C

so you can make your own arrangement, using the skeletal tune, the variations I do, or others. My setting goes from a simple approach through progressively more complex variations, using most of the common devices, hammers, pulls, slides, drop-thumb, and the rippling IPIT, as in the 1st two measures of Pt. II, where the index lead is followed by a pull-off from the touched but not fretted 1st string, followed by the same note struck by the index, and finally kicked off by the thumbed 5th string.

Old Joe Clark

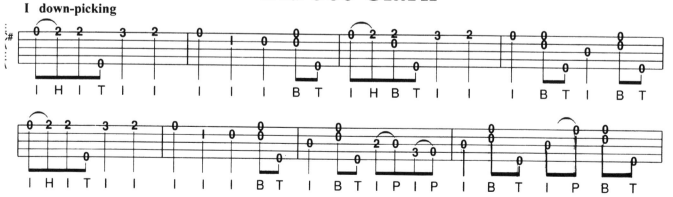

Traditional; arranged by Art Rosenbaum
Copyright © 1975 Kicking Mule Publishing

23

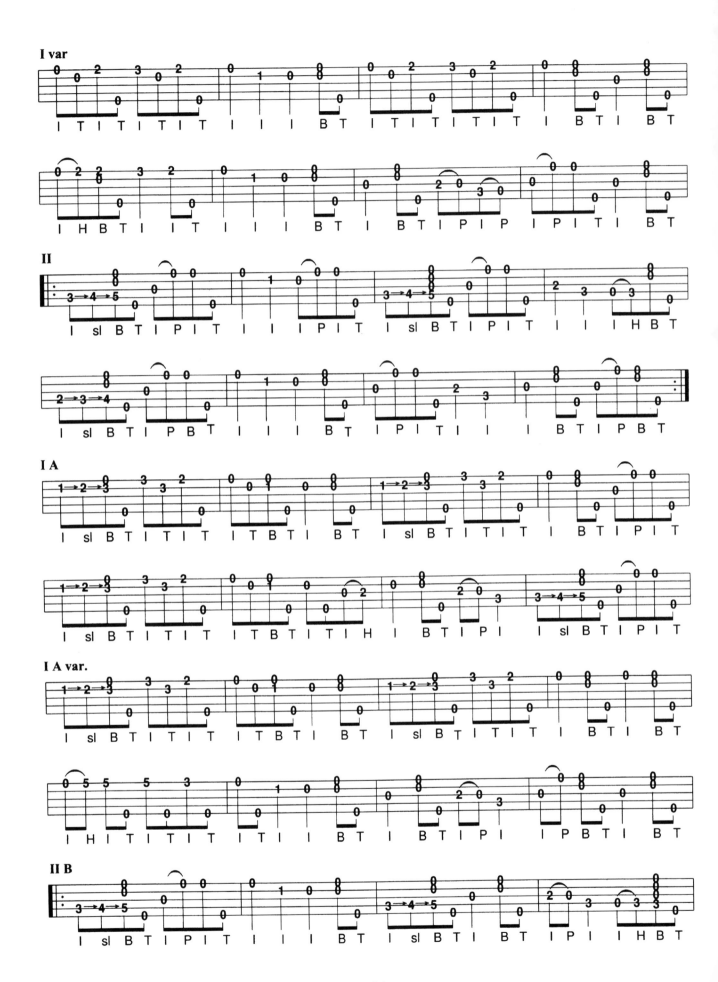

Old Joe Clark (cont.)

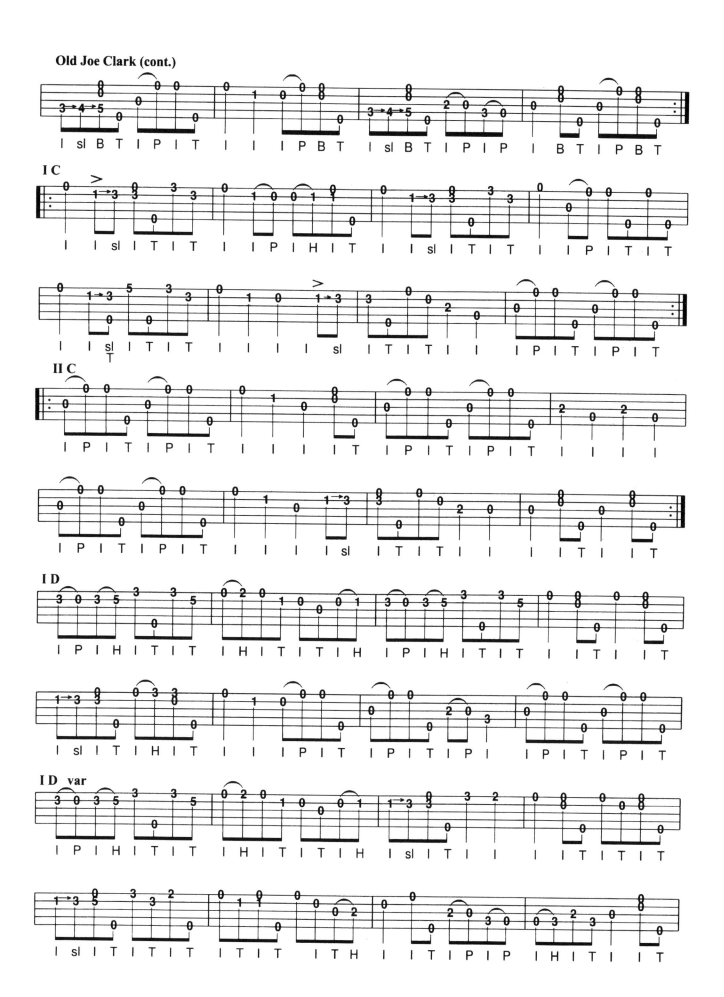

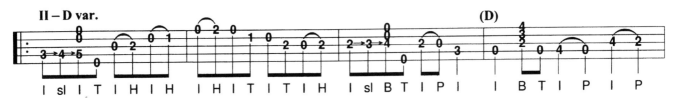

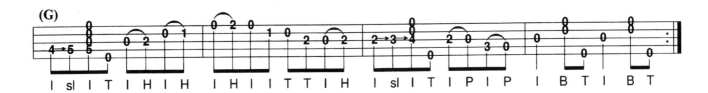

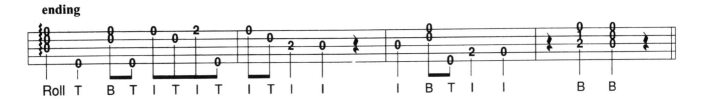

WATERBOUND

This vignette of a mountain frolic cut off from the rest of the world by a flash flood of a creek-bed road, but carrying on in all its hilarity until day, was played by the Bogtrotters and others of the Galax, Virginia area. They did a string band treatment of a play party ditty.

TUNING: ^{G}DGBD   (G tuning)

PICKING: Down-picking. At times the secondary beat, the beat after the index lead is a brush, at times another note struck by the index. There is a lot of syncopation in this tune, i.e. the transition between measures 8 and 9, where the accented note falls at the end of the measure rather than at the beginning of measure 9.

Waterbound

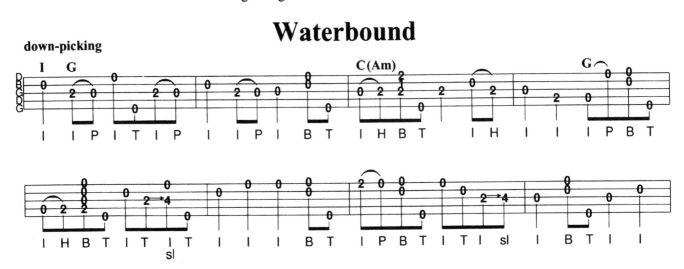

Traditional; arranged by Art Rosenbaum

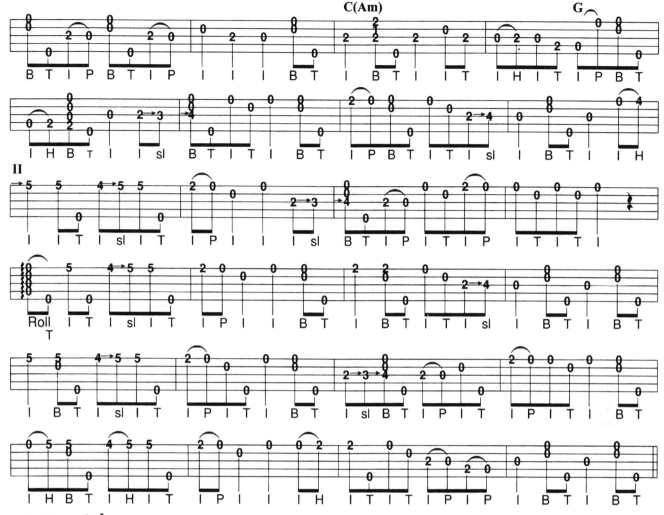

verses sung to I

1) Chicken's crowin' in the old plowed field (3x)
   down in North Carolina.

   Chorus: Waterbound and I can't go home (3x)
             have to stay till mornin'

2) Nick and Charlie left to go home (3x)
   before the water rises.

3) Water's up and I can't get across (3x)
   I'll ride the old white hoss.

   Chorus: Waterbound and I can't go home (3x)
   have to stay till mornin'

4) The old man's mad but I don't care (3x)
   just so I get his daughter.

5) If he don't give her up I'm gonna run away (3x)
   down in North Carolina.

   Chorus: Waterbound and I can't go home (3x)
             down in North Carolina

HAD A LITTLE FIGHT IN MEXICO

These are the verses sung by Jean Ritchie, but they don't differ greatly from other texts of this song, widely sung in the Appalachians a generation ago. Singing play party songs such as this was popular in communities where there were religious feelings against dancing to fiddles and banjos. But occasionally they were taken up by instrumentalists.

TUNING: GDGCD The "mountain minor" or "sawmill" tuning, used for pieces in a minor mode such as PRETTY POLLY, THE CUCKOO, and EAST VIRGINIA. From the G tuning, raise the 2nd string 1/2 tone (1 fret), and check against the 3rd string stopped at the 5th fret. (On the recording the banjo is tuned a bit below pitch.)

PICKING: Down-picking. The banjo played on the recording is a fretless one, accounting for the characteristic sound with smooth slides. The TAB is written in fret positions, and the tune could be played on a fretted instrument. There are many IPIT's used, creating a rippling second drone effect. Occasionally the thumb drops to the 2nd or 3rd strings, not nearly so common as drop-thumb to the 2nd string in traditional playing.

Had a Little Fight in Mexico

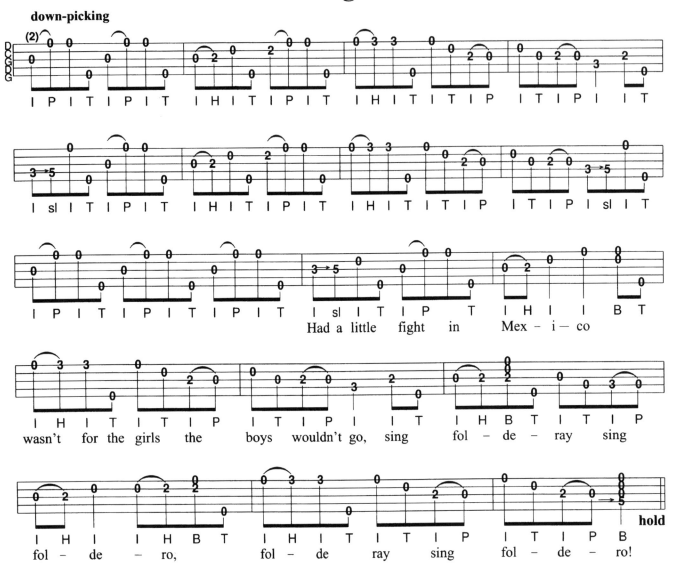

Traditional; arranged by Jean Ritchie
Copyright © 1975 Jean Ritchie

1) Had a little fight in Mexico
      wasn't for the girls the boys wouldn't go
         sing fol-de-ray, fol-de ro,
         fol-de-ray sing fol-de ro.

2) Had a little trouble down t' other end of town,
      nobody kilt but a man knocked down
         sing, etc.

3) Got to the place where the blood was shed,
      girls move back and the boys step ahead
         sing, etc.

4) Had a little fight in Mexico
      wasn't for the girls the boys wouldn't go
         sing, etc.

28

Mabel Cawthorn, Carnesville, GA 1983 — *Photo Margo Newmark Rosenbaum*

SALLY GOODIN

Sally Goodin is a square dance tune played throughout the South. This setting was adapted from the playing of the late Justus Begley, sheriff of Perry County, Kentucky. He was a great singer of old songs as well as a driving picker of breakdowns. The banjo is tuned GCGCD and is frailed in the rough and ready Kentucky manner. This style lacks some of the melodic complexity of the Virginia clawhammer picking but makes up for it in speed and verve.

TUNING: ᴬDADE   or the two-C tuning, capoed up a whole tone, with the 5th string tuned up to A.

PICKING: Down-picking. An exception to the usual downward attack occurs at the I' section where a downward brush is followed by the index sounding the strings as the hand moves UP, as in Pete Seeger's "whamming" approach. Kentucky mountain banjo pickers sometimes fill out the sound of their down-picking with notes hit on the up-swing. Here the contrast between the single note passages and the very full passages would be emphasized.

Sally Goodin

Traditional; arranged by Art Rosenbaum
Copyright © 1975 Kicking Mule Publishing

30

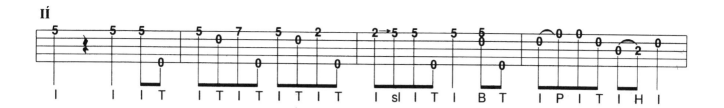

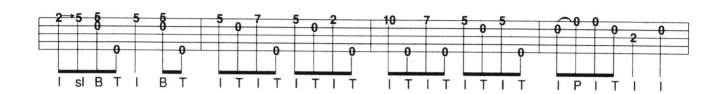

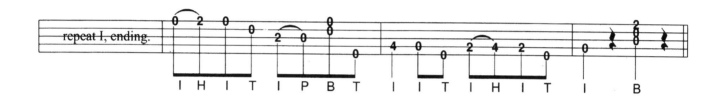

GRUB SPRINGS

I adapted this from a fiddle tune played by Mississippi fiddler W. E. Claunch on Library of Congress record L2.

TUNING: ^{A}DADE   or two-C (^{G}CGCD), capo'd up.

PICKING: Down-picking. There are many drop-thumb notes to fill out the melody. In II, the left hand must move rapidly from the F formation (see notes to DRY AND DUSTY) up the fingerboard, and back. This position is used in the final measure of I:

Grub Springs

Traditional; arranged by Art Rosenbaum
Copyright © 1975 Kicking Mule Publishing

GOIN' ACROSS THE SEA

I first heard this lyric piece played many years ago by Edward Ward, well-digger and banjo picker from central Kentucky who lived in my home town of Indianapolis. A few years later I heard versions from Shorty Sheenan and Dallas Henderson, also Appalachian musicians who had moved up to Indiana, and added some of their licks and verses to what I had been playing and singing. The present refrain was sung by Shorty and his wife, Juanita. A quintessential rendition by Uncle Dave Macon can be heard on County 521.

TUNING: ^{G}CGCD   (two-C)   These chord figures are used:

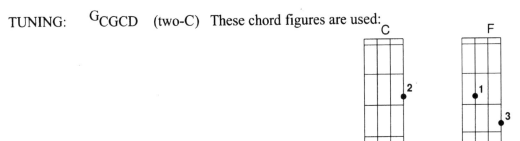

PICKING: Down-picking. There is a lot of melodic dropthumb. The rolls are produced by a raking of the backs of the finger nails across the strings and are here followed first by a hammered note on the 1st string, then by a thumbed 5th string note, by a pull-off of the 1st string note which has been held down.

32

Ola Belle Reed, Mariposa Folk Festival, Toronto, mid–1970s — *Photo Margo Newmark Rosenbaum*

Goin' 'Cross the Sea

Traditional; arranged by Art Rosenbaum
Copyright © 1975 Kicking Mule Publishing

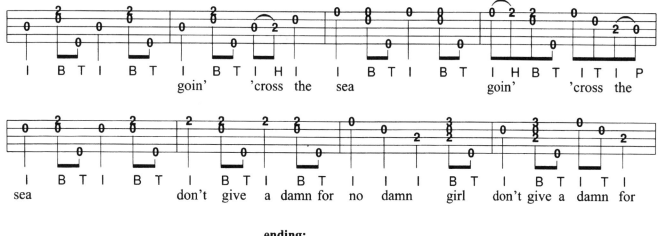

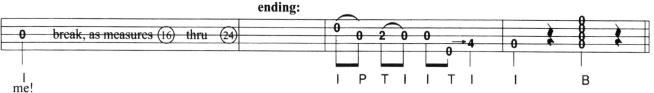

ending:

1) Won't you come and go, won't you come and go?
   Can't you change a nickel,
   can't you change a dime?
   Can't you go to Tennessee and
   change your name to mine?

   Chorus: Goin' across the sea, goin' across the sea,
           Don't give a damn for no damn girl
           Don't give a damn for me.

2) Wish I had a nickel,
   wish I had a dime,
   wish I had a pretty little girl to
   talk to all the time.

3) Last time I saw her, she's
   standin' in the door,
   shoes and stockings in her hands,
   feet all over the floor.

   Chorus:

4) The higher up the cherry tree
   the riper grows the cherry,
   the more you hug and kiss the girls
   the sooner they get married.

   Chorus:

5) If I had a needle and thread
   Fine as I could sew,
   I'd sew them pretty girls to my side,
   Down the road I'd go!

   Chorus:

Bobby and Georges Childers, Pickens Co. GA — *Photo Margo Newmark Rosenbaum*

D MEDLEY - -
MISSISSIPPI SAWYER,
OLD MOLLY HARE,
SOLDIERS' JOY

Here are three well known dance tunes, worked out in a fairly complex, highly melodic drop-thumb style. The first is an American creation, the other two come out of the British fiddle repertoire. Peter Hoover calls this style "Face of the Mountain", as it is "Best Developed Along the Topographic Front of the Blue Ridge..." He points out that the style developed in the fiddle by combination where the fiddle always carried the lead, and the banjo provided "rhythmic accompaniment as well as some snatches of the melody line." The banjo can carry these tunes alone, but you should team up with a fiddle if you want to get the most out of this style. My playing of "Mississippi Sawyer" is indebted to Wade Ward for the modal twist to the melody, and a recent re-listening to Hobart Smith's "Soldier's Joy" revitalized my attitude toward this standard (He played it in the standard C tuning G-CGBD). As fiddle always. plays these in D, the banjo picker accommodates by tuning his or her instrument up (The Traditional Practice) or by using a capo.

TUNING ^{A}DADE   or two-C tuning (^{G}CGCD), capoed up a whole tone, to play in key of D.

PICKING:

Down-picking. These tunes use the whole bag of down-picking licks. As in OLD JOE CLARK, the variations become progressively more complex, so it might be wise to play the simpler forms of the tunes until you get the feeling of the structure and sense of each, then try more difficult variations, or some that you devise yourself. Note that in the 9th line of MISSISSIPPI SAWYER, the little finger hammers up to the 7th fret while the 1st and 2nd fingers are in this position:

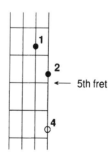

Then the figure is moved down two frets.

Generally, left hand noting is done with whatever finger(s) seem(s) most comfortable or efficient. The 3rd measure of OLD MOLLY HARE works around this fingering:

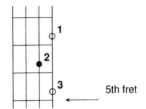

D Medley
Mississippi Sawyer

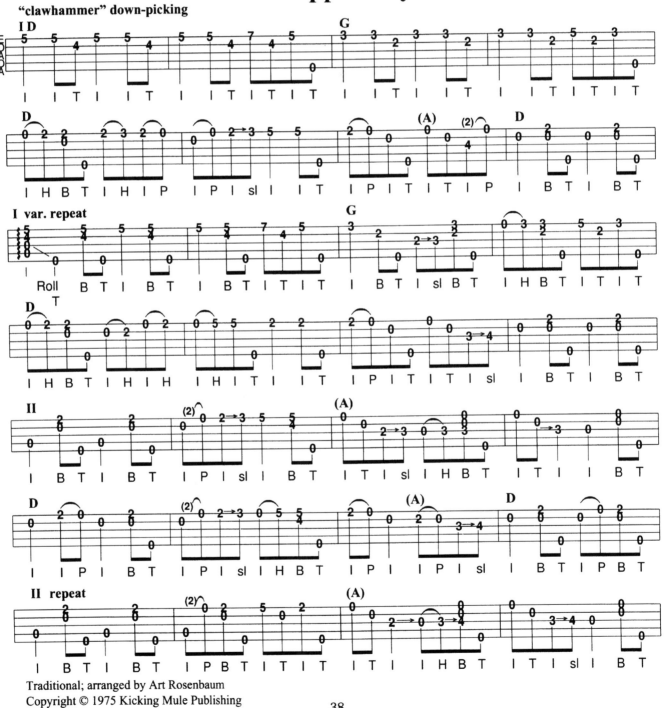

Traditional; arranged by Art Rosenbaum

D Medley, continued

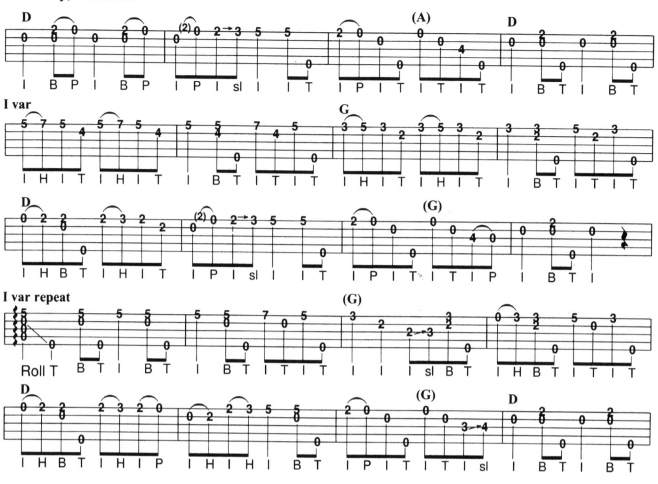

Old Molly Hare

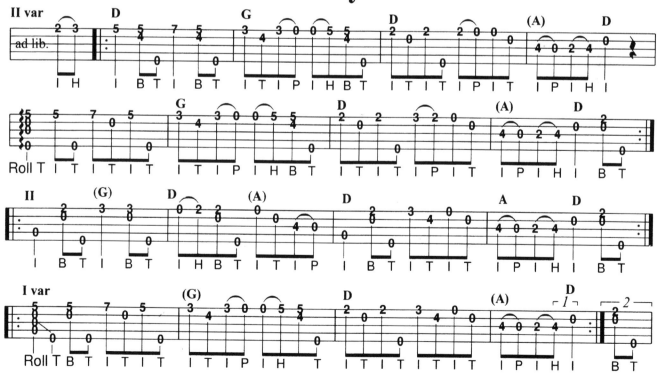

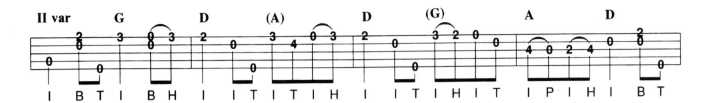

Soldiers' Joy

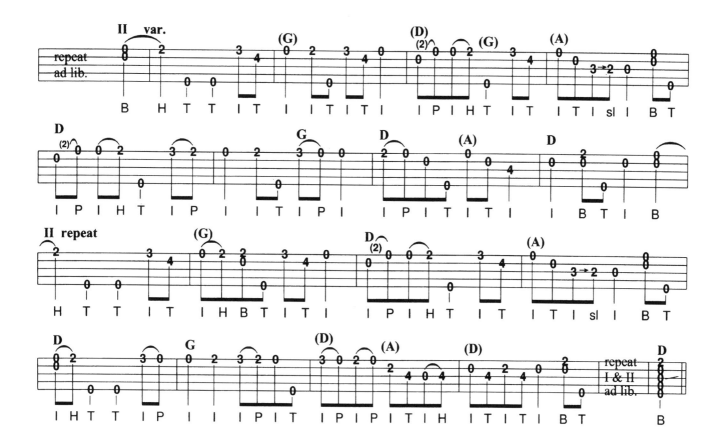

SANDY RIVER

I try to stay pretty close to the way Oscar Wright, of Princeton, West Virginia, plays this tune on County Records 717. Although "Sandy River" is a common fiddle tune, it would take a particularly adept fiddler to follow the banjo in this irregularly structured and unusual version...so much the better, as there should be some tunes that are not squared off in deference to ensemble playing but make their own idiosyncratic musical and expressive sense. The mood is intensified by the particularly "Lonesome" tuning, called and expressive sense. The "Last Chance" by the late Hobart Smith.

TUNING: GDGDE   or Hobart Smith's "Last Chance" tuning. From the tuning used in the previous tune (ADADE), run the two A's, the 5th and 3rd strings, down 1 tone (two frets). Tune the 3rd string to the 4th stopped at the 5th fret, the 5th string to the 1st stopped at the 3rd fret. Or tune the 5th and 3rd down from the corresponding two-C tuning, to play in F (FCFCD).

PICKING: Down-picking.   The structure of this tune is highly irregular. However, it is a veritable compendium of clawhammer down-picking licks and techniques, and shows the way a subtle melody can be wedded to the rhythmic punch delivered by the downward attack of the right hand.   There are slides up and down the fingerboard, the IPIT (index-pull-index-thumb) lick, melodic drop-thumb (note that in measures 6 and 9 the thumb drops first the 5th, then to the 2nd string, a reverse of the usual order, but no more difficult to do and, in this case, necessary for the tune). Often the pattern is ITIT instead of IBT, with the index occasionally hitting a lower string the second time in the sequence, again for reasons of melody.

Sandy River

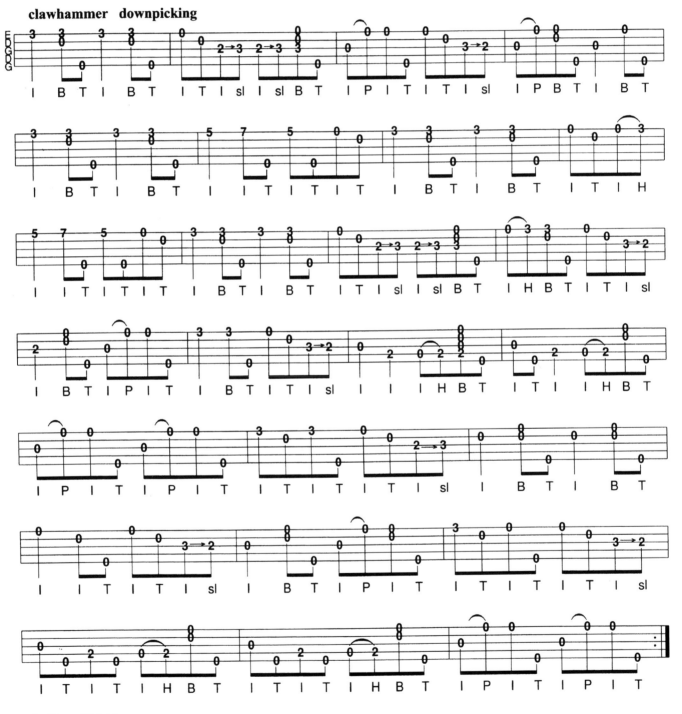

by Oscar Wright
Copyright © 1975 Oscar Wright

Kentucky 1970 — *Photo Margo Newmark Rosenbaum*

TENNESSEE LINE
HARD TIMES

This tune is of the widespread "Ruben" or "Train 45" family, but the text is a fragment of what must have been a longer ballad about a Moonshiner or "Blockader" named Roscoe Cherry. I got it from Edward Ward, one of the first old time banjo pickers I spent time learning from, first hand. He lived in my home town of Indianapolis but hailed from Kentucky and his picking, simple failing and two finger picking, was typical of that area.

TUNING: ECEGC   This is the open D tuning, tuned down a whole tone. To get into the open D tuning ($^{F\#}$DF#AD), in which you might want to try this tune, start with the open G tuning (^{G}DGBD), as in GREY EAGLE. Then drop the 3rd string 1/2 tone, to F#, and match with the 4th string stopped at the 4th fret; drop the 2nd a whole tone, to A—match with the 3rd at 3; and tune the 5th down 1/2 tone—match with the 1st string at 4.

PICKING: Down-picking. I have added Buell Kazee's technique of at times catching the inside strings with the BACK of the thumb-nail as the hand rises in the usual down-picking bounce. This is a little tricky at first, but adds a possibility of a second drone or some nice syncopation if some melodic elements are involved.

Tennessee Line Hard Times

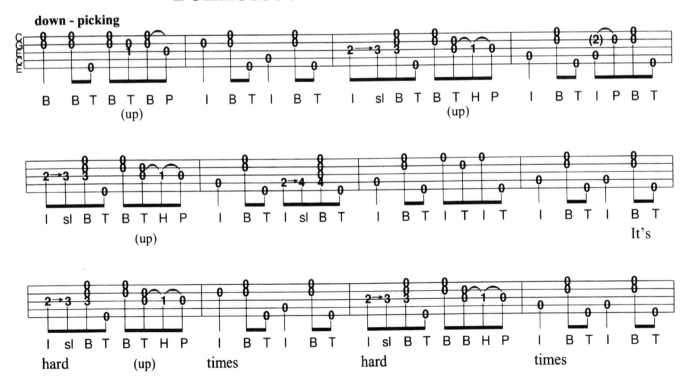

Traditional; arranged by Art Rosenbaum
Copyright © 1975 Kicking Mule Publishing

It's hard times, hard times,
Tennessee line hard times.

Well it's old Roscoe Cherry
With all the whiskey he could carry, and it's

It's hard times, hard times,
Tennessee line hard times.

Well he went down to Tennessee
Midst all the hail and rain,
Brought him back to old Kentucky
Wearin' the ball and chain, and it's

Hard times, hard times,
Tennessee line hard times.

OLD RUBEN

This is an instrumental version of a banjo song that mountain musicians took over from Black
railroad workers around the turn of the century. I use the D tuning (F#DF#AD), traditional for
the piece, and put in licks learned from Pete Steele, Riley Shelton and Cass Moore.

TUNING: F#DF#AD (D tuning)

PICKING: Down-picking, here done on the fretless banjo, but the TAB is noted
                    for the fretted banjo.   Note the drop-thumb passages with the lead on
                    the 2nd string and the thumb dropping to the 3rd, as well as the
                    measures like #4 where a brush of the 5th & 4th strings is used as a
                    lead instead of the usual index on one of the first four strings. See
                    Old Time Mountain Banjo (Oak, 1968) for more variations on this tune.

Uncle John Patterson, Gordon Tanner, Smokey Joe Miller, Dacula, GA -- *Photo by Margo Mewmark Rosenbaum*

Old Ruben

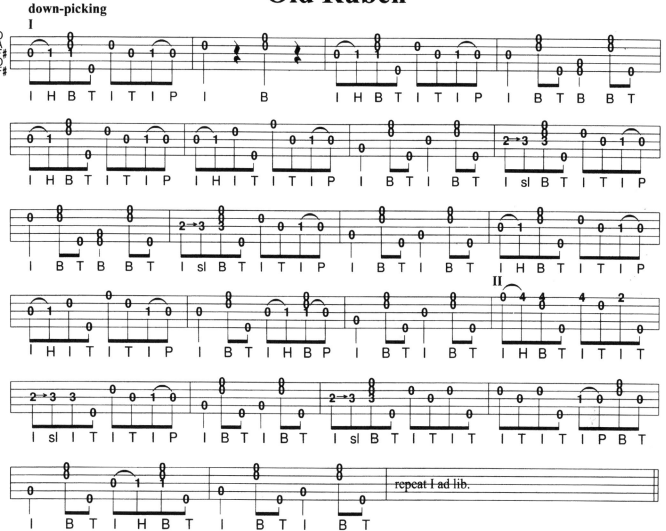

Traditional; arranged by Art Rosenbaum

Copyright © 1975 Kicking Mule Publishing

G MEDLEY —
HELL ON THE WABASH
SENECA SQUARE DANCE

Banjo pickers seldom seem to play medleys as fiddlers often do, but I arranged these two settings from fiddle tunes, and they seemed natural go togethers. "Hell On The Wabash" comes from the fiddle repertoire of Charlie Drollinger of Iowa City. He learned it from his father and uncles after the turn of the century, and often had to back them up on it on the 5-string banjo (chorded and picked 3-finger style). "Seneca Square Dance" is another West of the Mississippi piece. It appears in Ira Ford's *Traditional Music in America*: Joel Shimberg suggests that it is a cousin of "Shoot the Turkey Buzzard".

TUNING: GDGBD (open G)

PICKING: Down-picking. Closely based on fiddle melodies, drop-thumb, hammers, and pulls, etc., are used to provide a flowing melodic line. These chord figures occur in HELL ON THE

WABASH, and are the principal chords in this key:

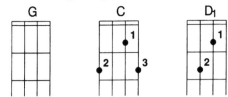

The "fine" or high second part of SENECA SQUARE DANCE works around this fingering:

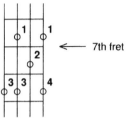

← 7th fret

G Medley
Hell on the Wabash

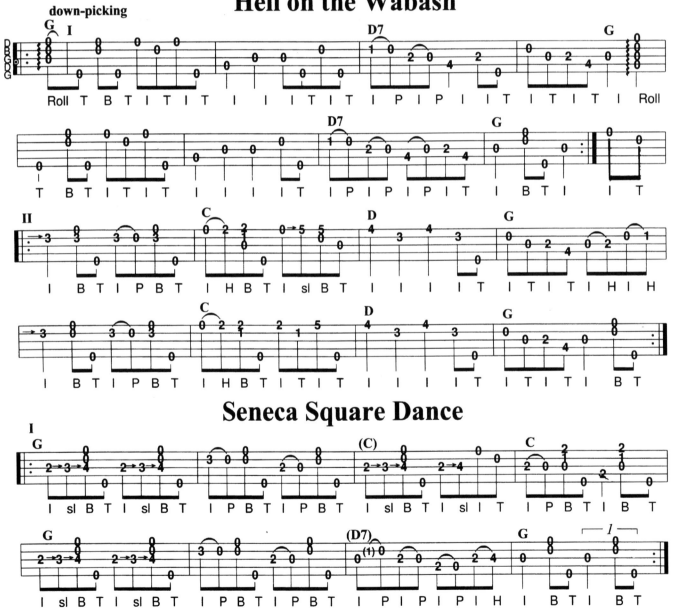

Seneca Square Dance

Traditional; arranged by Art Rosenbaum

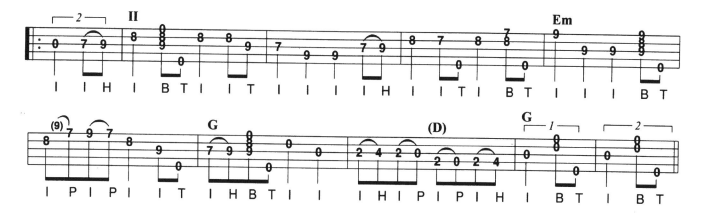

G MEDLEY —

CHARMING MOLLY BRANIGAN, TEETOTALER'S FANCY

These are two Irish reels that I worked up in claw-hammer style. I first heard them played by the Hoosier fiddler, John W. "Dick" Summers. He called them "Mother Flannigan" and "Darkey's Dream". To complicate the matter further, the first tune is often called "Green Fields of America".

TUNING: GDGBD   (open G)

PICKING: Down-picking.   Again the approach emphasizes melody.   The triples, produced by two consecutive hammer-ons, are borrowed from Irish fiddle music.   See the previous tunes for the chords in G. In TEETOTALER'S FANCY, the following E minor chord is used:

Charming Molly Brannigan

Traditional; arranged by Art Rosenbaum
Copyright © 1975 Kicking Mule Publishing

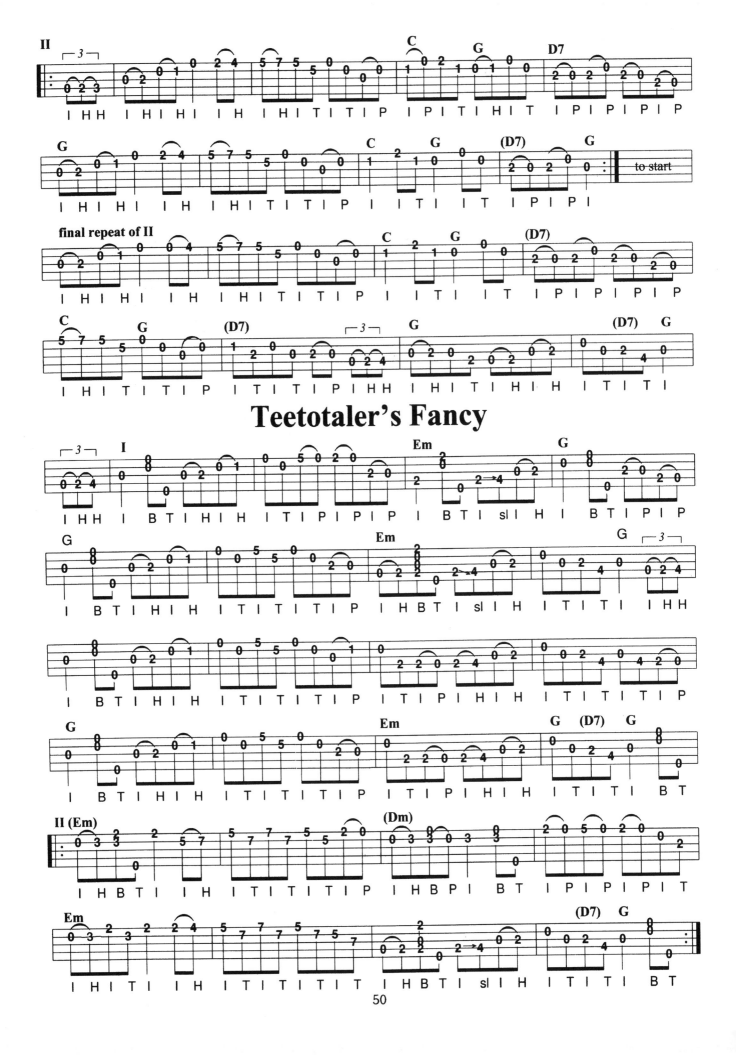

Teetotaler's Fancy

Vaughn Eller, Lawrence Eller, Ross Brown, Upper Hightower, Towns Co. GA 1979
— *Photo Margo Newmark Rosenbaum*

JOHN BROWN'S DREAM

In some forms called "Little Rabbit", this is a classic clawhammer tune from the Mt. Airy, North Carolina region in a breakdown style that ideally pairs the banjo with fiddle. A driving syncopated rhythm is not sacrificed to the pushing out of the melody. I first heard this in the '50s played on both the banjo and fiddle by Cecil Rhodes, a migrant farm worker from Tennessee who was camping with his family in the Michigan Orchards (he called it "Jeff Davis' Dream"). Since then, I have heard it played by Tommy Jarrell (he tunes his 4th string down an octave from the 3rd as I do here); by Fred Cockerham, on fretless banjo (C. F. my transcription in *Old Time Mountain Banjo*). Tommy Jarrell's father, Ben Jarrell, recorded with DA Costa Woltz's Southern Broadcasters in the '20s and a reissue of Woltz's superb performance can be heard on County 524.

TUNING: ^{A}AAC#E This is the tuning Tommy Jarrell used for this piece. It is sometimes simply called "low bass." The banjo is tuned to open A (as in OLD JOE CLARK), or capo'd up a tone from open G. Then the 4th string is lowered until it is an octave lower than the 3rd string, two octaves lower than the 5th.

PICKING: Down-picking. Let the notes struck on the lowered bass string resound under the treble melody picked on the high strings.

See OLD TIME MOUNTAIN BANJO (Oak, 1968), for a fretless banjo version of this tune.

John Brown's Dream

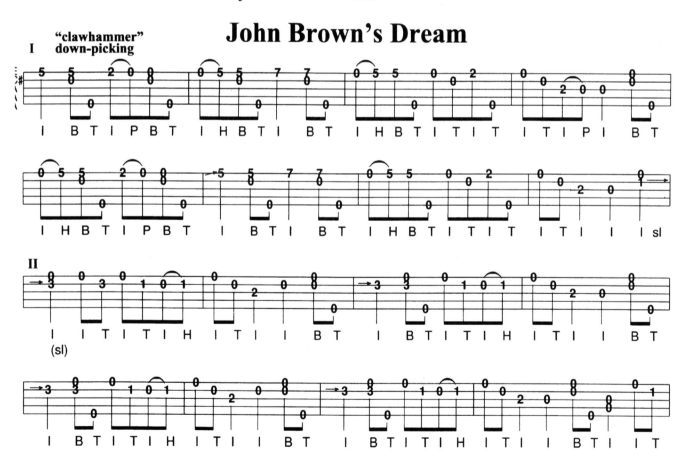

Traditional; arranged by Art Rosenbaum
Copyright © 1975 Kicking Mule Publishing

52

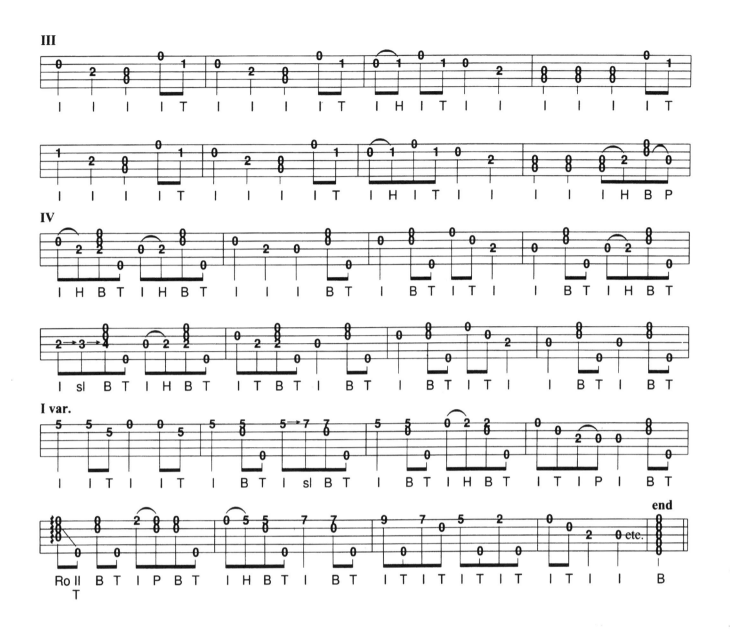

JOHN HENRY

Very frequently this song is played on the guitar in bottleneck, knife or slide style. I worked it out this way on the banjo, with a harp part thrown in. Tuning: ^{A}AAC♯E (or ^{G}GDBD, capo'd up 2 frets, 5th string tuned up a tone to A).

TUNING: ^{A}AAC♯E   This is the same tuning as that for JOHN BROWN'S DREAM. The equivalent in G would be the open G tuning with the 4th string dropped to a low G.

high break

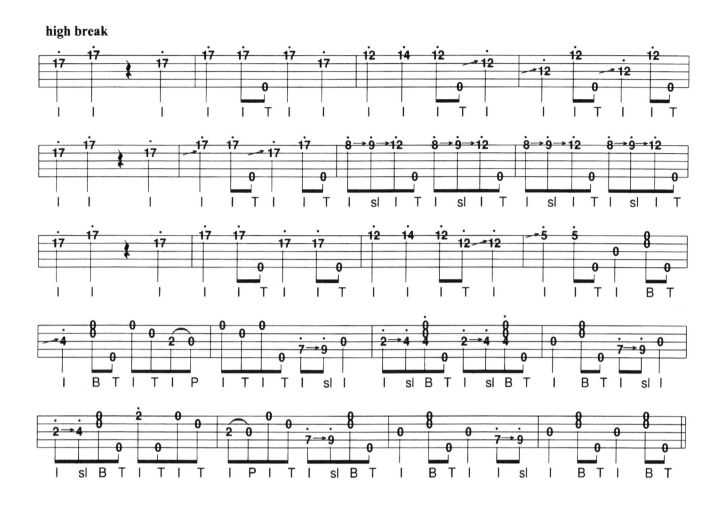

1) When John Henry was a little bitty boy
   No bigger than the palm of your hand,
   He picked up a hammer and a little piece of steel,
   Said "I'm gonna be a steel drivin' man,
   Gonna be a steel drivin' man."

2) When John Henry was a little bitty boy,
   No bigger than the palm of your hand,
   He looked up at his papa and said:
   "I'm gonna be a steel-drivin' man,
   I'm gonna be a steel-drivin' man."

3) Well John Henry said to his shaker:
   "Shaker, you better pray,
   For if I miss this little piece of steel,
   Tomorrow be your buryin' day,
   Tomorrow be your buryin' day,"

4) They put John Henry on the right hand side,
   Steam drill on the left,
   He drove so hard that he broke his poor heart,
   Hammered his fool self to death,
   Hammered his fool self to death.

5) Well some say he come from Cuba,
   And some say he come from Spain,
   But I say he come from a hard-rock levee camp,
   For steel-drivin' John Henry was his name,
   Steel-drivin' John Henry was his name.

COTTAGE IN THE GROVE

I adapted this arrangement from Jim Lucas' banjo setting of a rare fiddle tune.

TUNING: ^{A}EADE   Mountain minor, or "sawmill" tuning, here tuned or capo'd up to the key of A minor, though the G minor form (^{G}DGCD) could be used.

PICKING: Down-picking. Note the many melodic drop-thumbs on the 3rd and 4th strings. A small number in the TAB preceding a held hammered note indicates a grace note, a hammered rather than a sliding attack on a principal accent.

Cottage in the Grove

Traditional; arranged by Art Rosenbaum

MEDLEY--
STONY POINT,
BUCK CREEK GIRLS,
HARLAN COUNTY FAREWELL TUNE

There is a traditional practice where the banjo is tuned to a minor mode, usually C minor, A minor, but it is noted so as to produce a major chord, F or G... This, especially when the major key is G, permits the banjo to play along with a fiddle using some hammered and pulled notes not possible in standard open G, and keeps the instrument tuned high, so that the banjo picker is not forced to tune down when the fiddler throws in a tune in G amongst several in D, A, or minor.The first two tunes in this group are derived from the British American "Pigtown Fling" Family. "Stony Point" is a melodic clawhammer reworking of some fiddle versions I have heard. "Buck Creek Girls" is a more rhythmic treatment in the Kentucky Style (my playing derives from Pete Steele's, and a good performance by Banjo Bill Cornett can be heard on Folkways 2317). The final piece, according to Pete Steele, was played at the time of the first World War by a young Harlan County, Kentucky, draftee for his friends and kin who had come to see him off at the railway depot in Harlan. "This is my farewell Tune", he told them, "Because I don't believe I'm coming back." The conductor held the train up until the raucous breakdown was finished, the train pulled out, and the soldier never did return to his native hills.

TUNING: GEADE   This is essentially the A minor form of the mountain minor tuning, with the 5th string tuned down a whole tone, to match with the 1st string noted at the 3rd fret. Other variants would leave the 5th string at A, or tune it up (if it will stand the tension without breaking) to B. The following chord forms can be used to play in G in this tuning, in F in the G minor equivalent tuning, a whole tone lower:

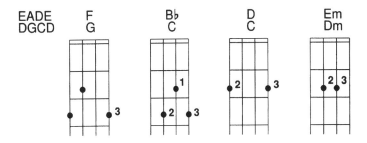

57

PICKING: Down-picking, working from the above (particularly the first) chord formations. STONY POINT requires a more sparse, accurate striking of melody notes, BUCK CREEK GIRLS is fuller and highly rhythmic. The second part of HARLAN COUNTY FAREWELL TUNE has a lick that involves a simultaneous drop-thumb and hammered note, creating a richness of tone note to be created otherwise. Pete Steele took special pains to show me this device.

Medley Stony Point

Buck Creek Girls

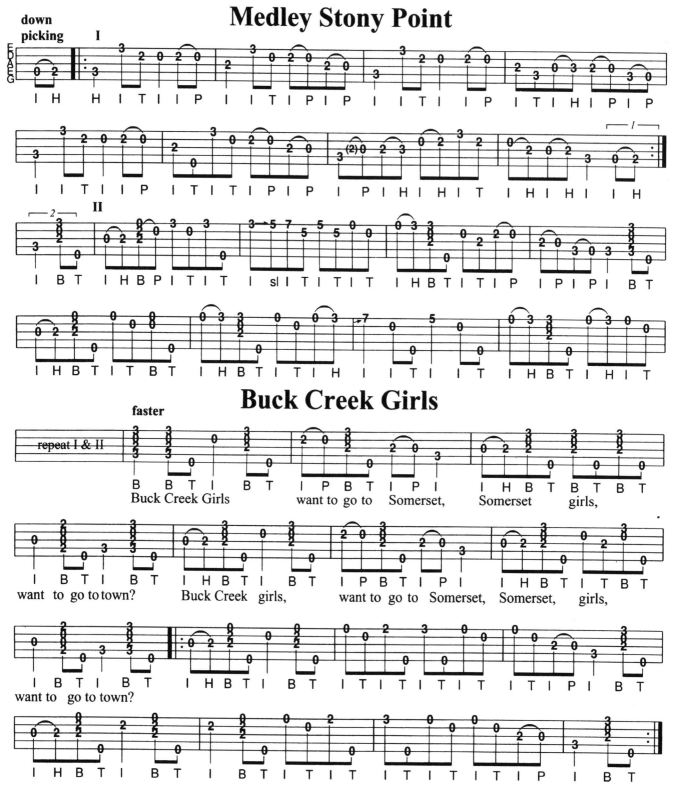

Traditional; arranged by Art Rosenbaum

Harlan County Farewell Tune

ARKANSAS TRAVELER

This is a fairly fancy arrangement of a well known tune, one that has many traditions and even a famous folk drama associated with it. There is a lot of melodic drop thumb up and down the neck.

TUNING: ^{A}DAC#E This is the standard C tuning (^{G}CGBD), tuned or capo'd up a whole tone, to the key of D, 5th string tuned to A.

PICKING: Down-picking. The emphasis is on the fiddle melody, and most of the usual devices are used. For a transcription of Hobart Smith's version of the piece in this tuning, see my OLD TIME MOUNTAIN BANJO (Oak). The tune is often played in the D form of the two-C tuning: for TAB of two settings in this tuning, see Miles Krassen's CLAW-HAMMER BANJO (Oak), and Eric Muller and Barbara Koehler's FRAILING THE 5-STRING BANJO (Mel Bay).

The Arkansas Traveler

Traditional; arranged by Art Rosenbaum

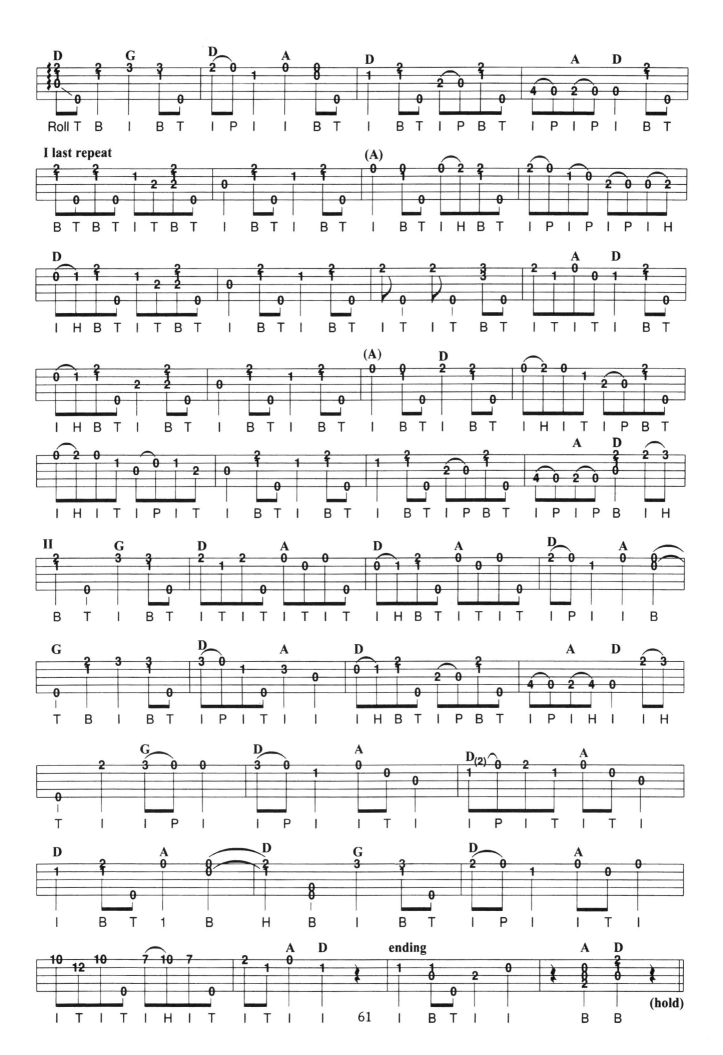

TURKEY IN THE STRAW

A popular standby as a fiddle or banjo tune, or a song. My father sang a verse about "Stinky Bill" to the melody. I play a melodic setting.

Following the lead of Dick Summers, I have mixed in a bit of the related piece "Natchez Under the Hill".

TUNING: ^{A}DAC♯E or the standard C tuning (^{G}CGBD), capo'd up a whole tone, as in preceding tune.

PICKING: Down-picking, with much melodic drop-thumb and hammered and pulled notes to fill out the melody. The following chord positions are used:

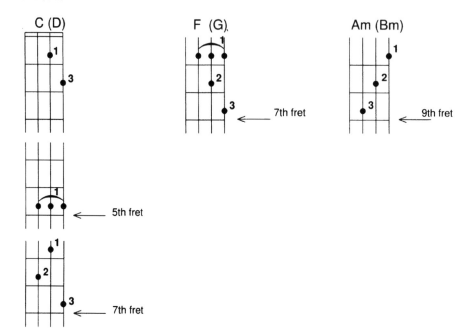

Turkey in the Straw

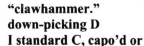

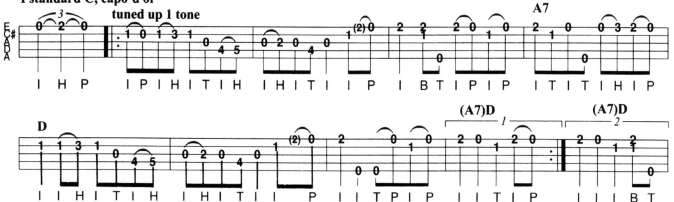

Traditional; arranged by Art Rosenbaum
Copyright © 1975 Kicking Mule Publishing

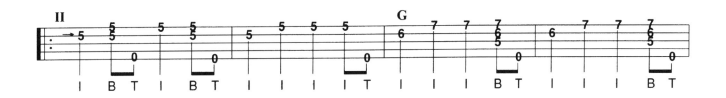

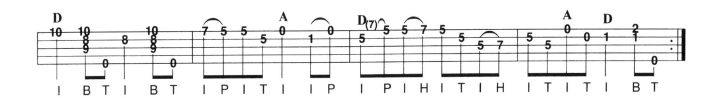

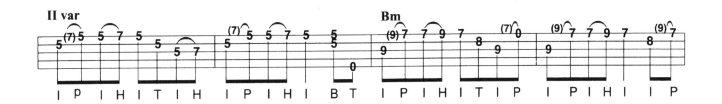

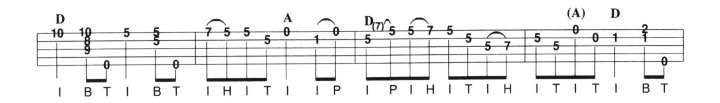

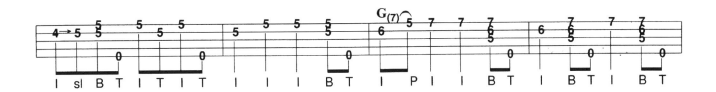

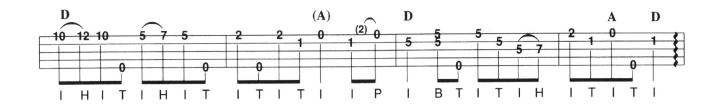

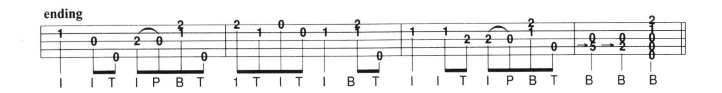

Elizabeth Cotten, c. 1974 — *Photo: Margo Newmark Rosenbaum*

UP - PICKING PIECES

Will Keys

SWEET NORA LEE

J. T. ADAMS, Indianapolis blues singer, played and sang this evocative vestige of a vast and largely lost body of jig tunes and banjo pieces that were commonly played by black southern musicians before the guitar began to supplant the banjo and fiddle as a folk instrument, and the blues eclipsed the older lyrics and ballads. He learned it as a boy in Morganfield, Kentucky, from his father whose banjo repertoire also included "Hop, John" and "Old Joe Clark".

TUNING: GDGBD   (open G tuning)

PICKING: Up - picking. The lead notes are picked UP, with the index finger, followed, most commonly, by a downward brush of the strings, and ended by the thumb on the 5th string. This is Pete Seeter's "basic strum", and it is less awkward at first than down - picking. The rhythm is ONE two - and, ($\quad$) ; if hammers or pulls are used, one - and two - and ($\quad$) . Here, there is no double - thumbing, as the thumb stays on the 5th string, but in the first two lines there is some sparse sketching out of the tunes with the thumb and index. In the second part, note that hammered notes often fall on strings other than the one previously sounded. Note also that a pulled note is sometimes used instead of the thumbed 5th for an off - beat.

Sweet Nora Lee

by J.T. Adams

SMOKY MOUNTAIN
CASS MOORE'S TUNE
GOIN' DOWN THE ROAD FEELIN' BAD

I met Cass Moore, a long-boned man from North Carolina who was up picking blueberries in Southern Michigan, in the summer of 1957. He would get me to pick a banjo tune for him to buckdance to, then he would take over the banjo and play a snatch of one tune or another. He was not a flashy picker, but he had plenty of musical passion in his soul and fingers, and he could sing with real conviction the song that has come to be the theme of the migrant farm workers.

TUNING: GDGBD   (open G tuning)

PICKING: Up - picking. The first of these tunes is very simple, a good learning piece for up - picking. Note that occasional notes are sounded by the thumb on the inside strings. In the second tune, the typical double thumbing sequence of ITIT, with the first thumbed note on the second, the second on the 5th string, occurs. A C chord is produced by the index finger barring the first three strings at the 5th fret.

66

Smoky Mountain Cass Moore's Tune

up - picking

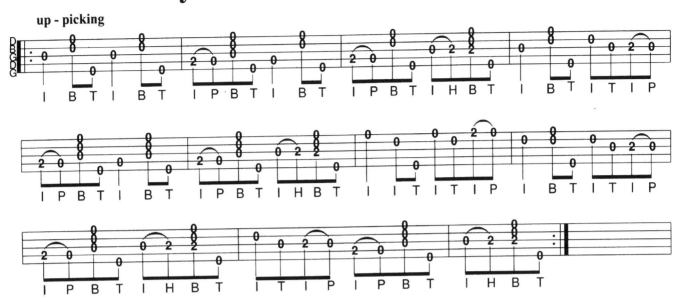

Goin' Down the Road Feelin' Bad

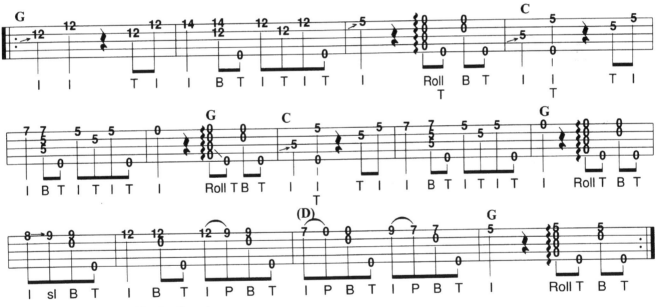

Traditional; arranged by Art Rosenbaum
Copyright © 1975 Kicking Mule Publishing

1) Goin' down the road feelin' bad (3x)
   Well I hain't gonna be treated this away.

2) Honey babe, you done me wrong (3x)
   Well I hain't gonna be treated this away.

3) Honey babe, you'll miss me when I'm gone (3x)
   Well I hain't gonna be treated this away.

4) Back, Back old freight train, get your load (3x)
   Well I hain't gonna be treated this away.

5) Goin' where them chilly winds dont't blow (3x)
   Well I hain't gonna be treated this away.

LITTLE BIRDIE

TUNING: ᴇCGAD   ("Little Birdie" tuning) From the standard C tuning, drop the 2nd
string a whole tone, to A (match to the 3rd string at 2nd fret); drop

the 5th string a tone and a half, to E (match to the 1st string at the 2nd fret). These chord positions are used:

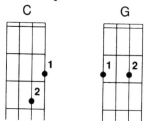

PICKING:
Up - picking. Watch for the spots where the thumb hits the 4th rather than the 5th string for a drone. This arrangement uses a good bit of of double - thumbing, and some choked notes, notes pushed to one side as they are picked.

Little Birdie

This way of tuning for and picking "Little Birdie" are pure Kentucky, though the song is known through-out the mountains. My version owes much to Pete Steele, particularly his break, where he very subtly uses the thumbed 4th string (instead of the 5th) as a drone; other ideas come from Willie Chapman's rendition on Folkways 2317. I think the verses strike just the right balance between lonely introspection and lyric invention.

up - picking
Intro & verse accomp.

Traditional; arranged by Art Rosenbaum
Copyright © 1975 Kicking Mule Publishing

68

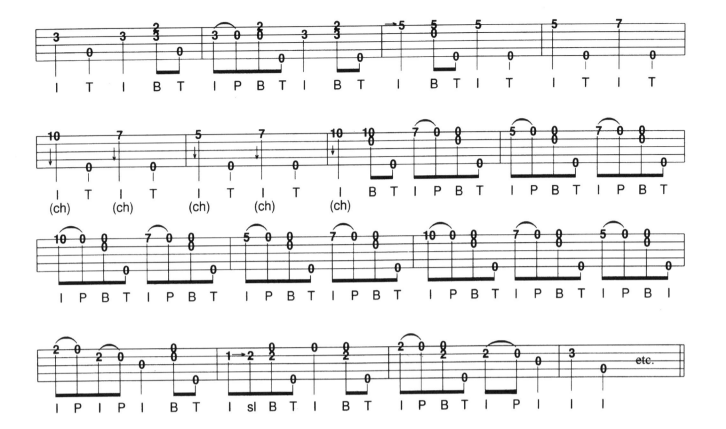

1) Little birdie, pretty birdie,
   come sing to me your song,
   got a short time to stay here
   and a long time to be gone.

2) Little birdie, little birdie,
   what makes you fly so high?
   you must have another true love
   way up yonder in the blue sky.

3) If I was a little birdie I'd not
   build a nest in the air, I'd build
   my nest in my true love's breast
   and roost in the locks of her hair.

THE GREEN BEDS

Cecil Sharp collected the text and this particularly fine modal melody to this English broadside ballad, sometimes called "The Saucy Sailor", in North Carolina. My banjo setting uses the approach of North Carolina pickers like Bascom Lamar Lunsford, Doc Watson and Wade Mainer, where the index finger picks up both the lead and second beats and the thumb hits off beats on the thumb string or moves into the inside strings for melodic double thumbing ... This works well where the banjo acts as both a rhythmic support and a second second voice to the singing.

TUNING: GDGCD   (Mountain minor)

PICKING: Up - picking. This form of up - picking is actually a type of two-finger picking, where the index takes the lead, and picks UP on the secondary beats, be they single notes, or chords of two or three notes.

69

The Green Beds

played in Cm (capo at 5)
up - picking

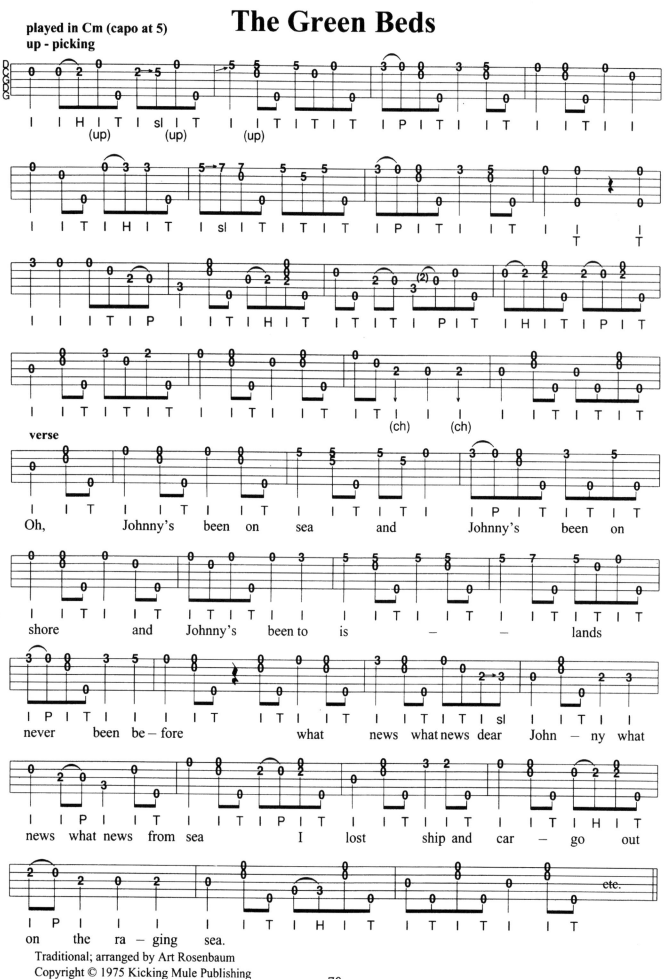

Traditional; arranged by Art Rosenbaum
Copyright © 1975 Kicking Mule Publishing

70

1) Oh Johnny's been on sea, Johnny's been on shore,
   And Johnny's been to islands never seen before.
   "What news, what news, dear Johnny, what news, what
                                    news from the sea?"
   "I lost ship and cargo out on the raging sea."

2) "Go bring your daughter Polly and set her down by me,
   We'll drink a melancholy and married we will be."
   "My daughter she is busy and can't come in to thee
   Except you wait an hour, it's one, two, and three"

3) Oh, Johnny's bein' drowsy, and hung down his head,
   He calls for a candle to light him to bed.
   "Our green beds are full, been full all this week,
   And so for your lodging you must go out in the street."

4) "Oh bring forth your reckoning book," Johnny he say,
   "And let me pay my reckoning bill before I go away."
   It then was twenty guineas the old woman did behold,
   And out of his pockets drew handfuls of gold.

5) And Polly running downstairs, a very pretty miss,
   She threw her arms around him for to hug and kiss.
   And the old woman, she vowed and she vowed in a rush,
   Said what she had been saying was said through a joke.

6) "Our green beds they are empty, been empty all this week
   Waiting for you and daughter Polly to take a pleasant sleep."
   "Oh you and your daughter Polly both deserve to be burned,
   Before I lodge in your green beds I'd lodge in a barn.

7) "Oh when I was a poor boy and for my lodging seek,
   I could not lodge in your green beds, had to lodge in the street.
   Oh now I have some money, so I'll roam the tavern free,
   With a bottle of peach brandy, and a pretty girl on each knee."

Uncle John Patterson, Georgia, c. 1980 — *Photo: Margo Newmark Rosenbaum*

TWO-FINGER PIECES

English Old-Time Banjo Gathering

MUSKRAT

"He/she can make a banjo talk" is an expression of approbation for a mountain musician. Vocal and instrumental ideas are intertwined in many cultures, among them the Afro-Amercian, from which the mountain banjo tradition springs. Here the fretless banjo first imitates or "mocks" the end of the vocal verse, then takes over. Merle Travis performs this on the guitar. I took some banjo ideas from a record by Land Norris of Georgia and some verses from Aunt Molly Jackson of Kentucky. Tuning: GCGCD.

TUNING: GCGCD   (Two-C tuning)

PICKING: Two-finger picking. For the most part, this is thumb-lead two-finger style, very useful for song accompaniments. The most common patterns are:

The first two measures demonstrate how a transition can be made from an index finger to a thumb lead.

The two-finger section is followed by a down-picking section, demonstrating how the melodic material can be treated in this style.

A fretless banjo is used on the disc, but the tune can, of course, be played on a fretted instrument.

Muskrat

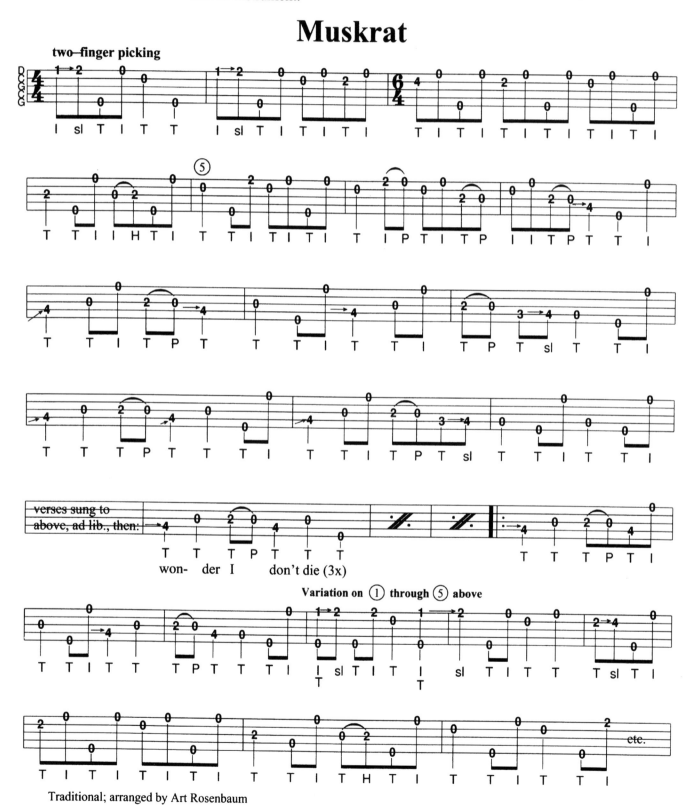

Traditional; arranged by Art Rosenbaum
Copyright © 1975 Kicking Mule Publishing

down–picking break

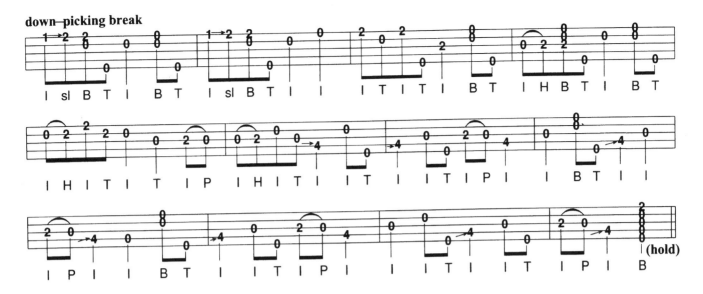

1) "Jaybird, Jaybird, what makes you fly so high?"
   "Been eatin' these acorns all my life,
   It's a wonder I don't die, wonder I don't die..." etc.

2) "Rattlesnake, rattlesnake, what makes your teeth so white?"
   "Been livin' in the bottom all my life,
   And I ain't done nothin' but bite, nothin' but bite..." etc.

3) "Muskrat, Muskrat, what makes your smell so bad?"
   "Been livin' in the water all my life,
   Till I'm mortified in my head, mortified in my head..." etc.

IN THE PINES

I learned most of these words from Riley Sheldon, although the verses are common property among Appalachian banjo pickers and singers. Bill Monroe does a particularly moving version of this railroader's lament. Two and three finger styles lend themselves more readily to 3/4 time than does down picking, although Ola Belle Reed has worked out some very solid clawhammer accompaniments for songs in this rhythm, following each lead with two rather than one brush thumb.

I B T B T

TUNING: F#DF#AD   (Open D, or "graveyard" tuning)

PICKING: Up-picking, then thumb-lead two-finger picking. This rather simple setting demonstrates how a melody can be picked out and a song accompanied in 3/4 time. The basic figure in up-picking is I, BT, BT; in two finger style.

I I

you can play T I T I T I or   T   T   T

Note that the index at times picks a note simultaneously with the completion of a slide or a hammer.

The one chord change from open D is an incomplete version of A

75

In the Pines

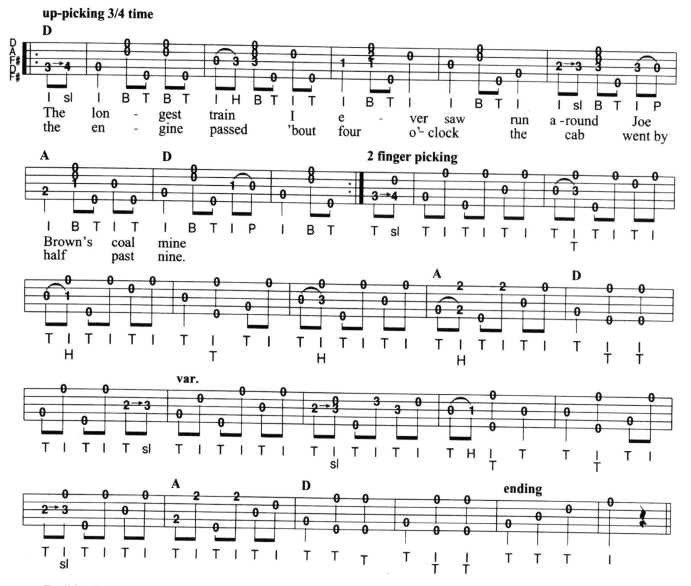

Traditional; arranged by Art Rosenbaum
Copyright © 1975 Kicking Mule Publishing

1) The longest train I ever saw
   run around Joe Brown's coal mine,
   the engine passed about four' o'clock
   the caboose went by half past nine.

   CHORUS: In the pines, in the pines
                where the sun never shines,
                I'll shiver when the cold wind blows.

2) Little girl, little girl, what have I done
   that you turn your back on me?
   I've killed no man, I've robbed no train,
   I've done no hangin' crime.

   CHORUS:

3) It's a long steel rail and a short cross-tie,
   I'm on my way back home.

THREE-FINGER PIECES

Mabel Cawthorn

COUNTRY BLUES

The blues is surely more a feeling than it is a special musical form, and the late Dock Boggs hit the mark in choosing this title for his most famous song; he recalled that it had been called the "Hustling Gamblers". It is a cousin of such "rounder" songs as "Darlin' Corey" and "Little Maggie", but Boggs' text and tune are perhaps the most poignant statement of the rough and rowdy boys of the southern mountains whose lives were rough and violent, whose love affairs were troubled and fleeting, whose preferred drink was moonshine whisky, and whose instrument was the 5-string banjo. Boggs' original Brunswick recording was reissued on the Folkways Anthology, Vol. III, and a later performance can be heard on Folkways 2351. See also Folkways 5458. Interviews with Dock Boggs, for his own story of learning this piece from itinerant Tennessee photographer and musician Homer Crawford, and of his playing it at his Brunswick audition and recording session in 1927.

TUNING: $F\#$CGAD   This is one of the D tunings favored by Dock Boggs (the other is $F\#$DGAD). From the open D tuning, raise the 3rd string to G, a whole tone, and lower the 4th string to C, a whole tone down. The lowered 4th string permits the evocative hammer that can be heard in the tuning measure on the record, and which occurs throughout the song.

PICKING: Three–finger style. Boggs' accompanyment is based on a simple roll using the thumb, index, and middle fingers, TIMI, often with a hammered note coinciding with the first index note-- the   first measure of the tag break, or the next to last measure in the TAB, illustrate the basic lick. Occasionally melody notes are worked in. My "verse or break" section is a bit more elaborate than Boggs' original.

Country Blues

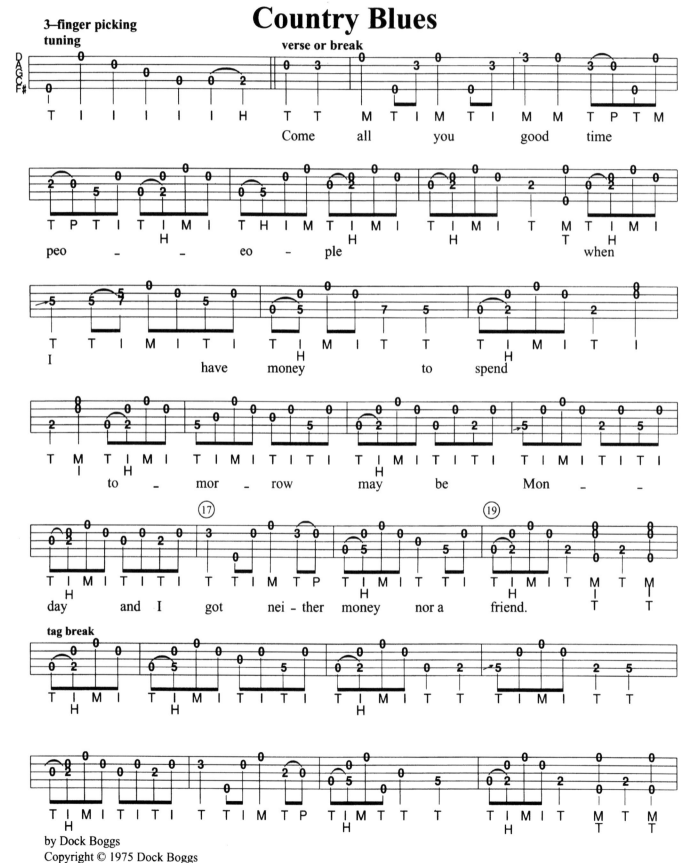

by Dock Boggs
Copyright © 1975 Dock Boggs

78

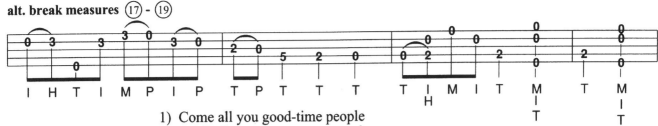

1) Come all you good-time people
      While I've got money to spend;
      Tomorrow may be Monday,
      And I haven't got a dollar nor a friend.

2) When I had plenty of money, good people,
      My friends was standin' around.
      Just as soon as my pocket book was empty
      Not a friend on earth to be found.

3) I gambled all over Kentucky, good people,
      And I gambled all the way to Spain.
      Now I'm goin' back to old Kentucky
      For to gamble my last card game.

4) The last time I seen my little woman, good people,
      She had a wine glass in her hand,
      She was drinkin' down her troubles
      With a low-down sorry man.

5) Oh my Daddy taught me plenty, good people,
      My mamma taught me more- -
      That if I didn't quit my rowdy ways
      Have trouble at my door.

6) I wrote my woman a letter, good people,
      I told her I's in jail.
      She wrote me back an answer,
      Sayin' "Honey, I'm a-coming for your bail."

7) All around this old jail house I'm layin', good people,
      Forty dollars won't pay my bail.
      Corn whiskey has surrounded my body, good people,
      Pretty women are a troublin' my mind.

8) Give me corn bread when I'm hungry, good people,
      Corn whiskey when I'm dry,
      Pretty women a-standin' around me,
      Sweet heaven when I die.

9) If I'd-a listened to my mamma, good people,
      I wouldn't be here today,
      But drinkin' and a-shootin' and a-gamblin',
      At home I cannot stay.

10) Go dig a hole in the meadow,
      Go dig me a hole in the ground;
      Come around all you good people
      And see this poor rounder go down.

11) Whem I am dead and buried
      With my pale face turned to the sun,
      You can come around and mourn, little woman,
      And think on the way you have done.

GOT A LITTLE HOME TO GO TO

This seems to be a West-of-the-Mississippi piece, known from Oklahoma (see *The Fiddle Book* by Marion Thede, Oak, 1968) up through the Ozarks and into Southern Iowa. The banjo tuning for it has a resonant bass string to set against the high figures and chromatic chimes. I pick it in both three-finger and down-picking style.

TUNING: GGGAD This is Wade Ward's "Fox Chase" tuning or Rufus Crisp's "Brighter Day" tuning. From the G tuning, the 2nd string is tuned down a whole tone, to A, and the 4th string is tuned an octave lower than the 3rd string; 2 octaves lower than the 5th. When tuned correctly, the 4th string, stopped at the 12th fret, should match the 3rd.

PICKING: Three-finger style, then down-picking. This setting is a hybrid old-fashioned three-finger style; the thumb picking down, the index and middle fingers picking up. Several of the rolls involve the index on the 3rd, the middle on the wind strings. Note the chimes, produced by touching the flesh of the left hand fingers to the strings but NOT pushed down to the fret. The string is picked and immediately released by the left hand.

Got a Little Home to Go To

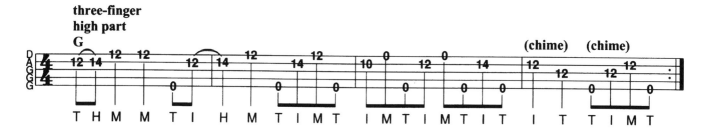

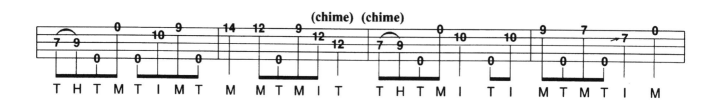

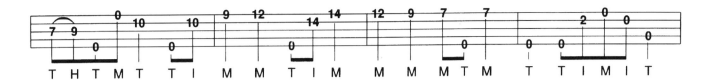

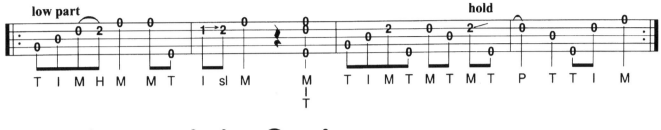

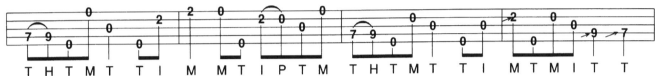

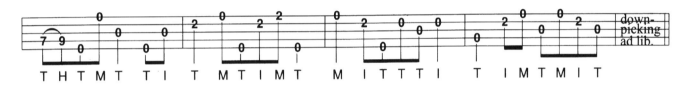

1) Saddle old Mike, I tell you,
   I'm goin' away to leave you,
   Way out to East Texas
   To eat corn bread and molasses-o.

   CHORUS: Got a little home to go to   (3X)
           And I'm gonna go there now.

2) Adam and Eve down in the garden.
   Studyin' human nature.
   Up jumped satan behind a stump,
   Hit 'Im in the face with a tater.

   CHORUS:

TEXAS RANGERS

This 19th century testimony of an anonymous young American caught in an unnecessary and brutal conflict continues to have meaning today. Most of the tunes and texts that have been recovered are fairly similar. I collected a typical version from Vergil Sandage of Doolittle's Mill, Indiana. I did like the final verses of a Kentucky version collected by the Lomaxes.

TUNING: GCGBE   A variant of the C tuning. I may have invented it. The 1st string is tuned up a whole
                        tone from D to E, making this the C chord:

PICKING: Three-finger style, thumb down, index and middle up. There are some passages where
                        the thumb and middle finger predominate, in a manner that owes much two-finger,
                        thumb lead approach. The melody is sung pretty much to the same setting used in
                        the melodic breaks.

Texas Rangers

Three-finger picking

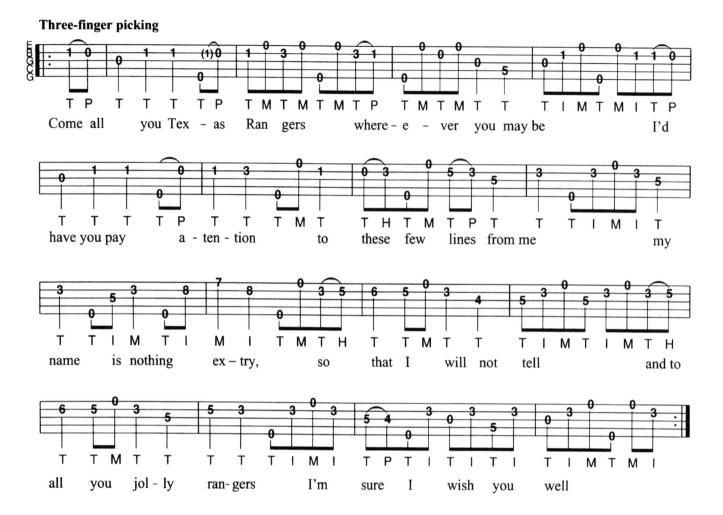

Traditional; arranged by Art Rosenbaum
Copyright © 1975 Kicking Mule Publishing

1) Come all you Texas Rangers whenever that you be,
   I'd have you pay attention to these few lines from me.
   My name is nothing extra, so that I will not tell,
   And to all you Jolly Rangers, I'm sure I wish you well.

2) 'Twas at the age of sixteen I joined this Jolly band,
   'Twas down in San Antonio, down by the Rio Grande.
   My Captain he informed me, perhaps he thought it right,
   "Before we reach the station, my boys we'll have to fight."

3) I saw the Indians coming, I heard them give a yell,
   My feelings at this moment no human tongue can tell.
   I saw the smoke a-rising, it reached up to the sky,
   I thought right at this moment, this is my time to die.

4) We fought them full five hours until the strife was o'er.
   The like of dead and wounded I never saw before.
   And as the sun was risin and the Indians they had fled,
   We loaded up our rifles and counted up our dead.

5) All of us are wounded, our noble Captain slain,
The sun was sadly shining across the bloody plain,
Six as bold young rangers as ever rode the West
Were buried by their comrades, with arrows in the breast.

6) "Twas then I thought of Mother who to me these words did say:
"To you they are strangers, at home you better stay."
I thought that she was childish and that she did not know,
My mind was bent on ranging, and I was bound to go.

7) I've know the fruits of rambling, I know its hardships well.
I've crossed the Rocky Mountains, rode down the streets of hell;
Been in the great Southwest where the wild Apaches roam,
And I tell you by experience, you better stay at home.

BLACK–EYED SUSIE

Ozark ballad singer Ollie Gilbert plays a few pieces on the banjo, and her simple and lonely way of picking this tune can give someone without much experience in 3-finger picking a notion of how to bring out a melody with a few simple rolls using the thumb, index, and middle fingers. The clawhammer variations use Kyle Creed's favored roll where the index strikes the 2nd and 1st string consecutively and is followed by the thumb on 5th string.

TUNING: GCGBD   (standard C)

PICKING: Three-finger style, followed by down-picking. The first section of this is an easy
study of the way melody can be achieved with some simple rolls, working from the
three chords in the key of C. The down-picking section begins with a lick favored
by Kyle Creed and other clawhammer players, two consecutive notes struck by the
back of the index in one continuous downward motion, followed by one or more
melody notes picked by the thumb on the 5th string.

Black–Eyed Susie

3 – finger

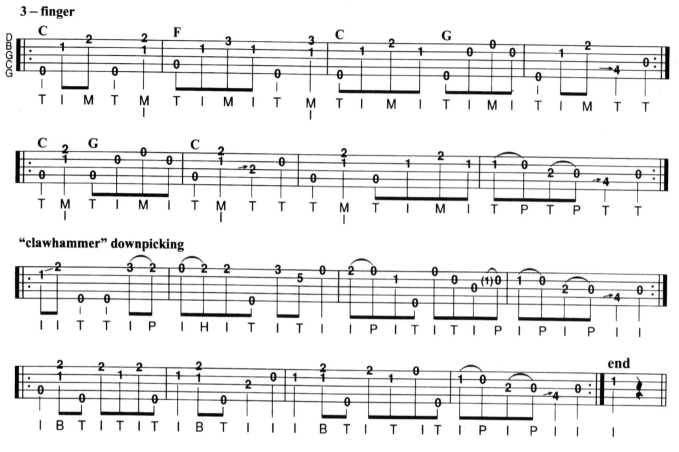

Traditional; arranged by Art Rosenbaum
Copyright © 1975 Kicking Mule Publishing

MAKE ME A PALLET

This fugitives' lament is another mountain adaptation of a Black folk song. I think, part of my version derives from Mainer's Mountaineers.

TUNING: ^{G}CFCD   (Two – C tuning)

PICKING: Three–finger picking, followed by down–picking. The three–finger style here is highly syncopated, and owes much to the approach of two–finger picking, though it is occasionally filled out by three–finger rolls.

Make Me a Pallet

3 – finger

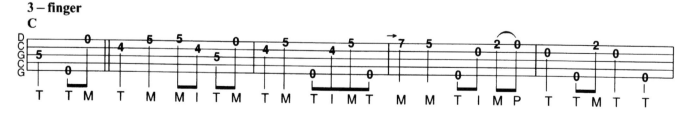

Traditional; arranged by Art Rosenbaum
Copyright © 1975 Kicking Mule Publishing

make me a pal – let down on your floor

Make me a pallet down on your floor,
Make me a bed right down by your door,
Make me a pallet down on your floor,

RISE WHEN THE ROOSTER CROWS

Uncle Dave Macon was certainly one of the greatest singers to the 5-string banjo. His huge and varied repertoire came not only from both black and white rural traditions, but from late 19th century southern "show business", the music of tent and medicine shows and vaudeville and minstrel performers. He reworked all this material in his highly personal and winning style as he became a radio and recording artist in the last of his long life. This song was originally recorded in 1926 (c.f. reissue on Vetco 101). Uncle Dave's three finger work, which I have slightly modified here, derives from minstrel styles...I added a few frail licks inspired by his syncopated style but which are not present on the original. Black and white musicians have had a hand in creating this parody of black gospel and secular folk song which, far from being offensive, is possessed of solid humor and high spirit.

TUNING: ADADF♯ From the tuning used in, say, the D MEDLEY (ADADE), raise the 1st string a whole tone (match with the 2nd string stopped at the 4th fret). This produces an open D chord. Or, from the corresponding two– C tuning (GCGCD), raise the 1st string to E, to produce the open C tuning. Then, to play in the key of D, use a capo at the 2nd fret and tune the 5th string up a tone, or use a 5th string capo or nail device at the 7th fret.

PICKING: Three-finger style, followed by down-picking variation. Some of Uncle Dave Macon's rolls and right hand techniques are used in this setting. Note the places where the fingers play three or four notes clustered in the time of one beat, at times concurrently with the completion of a sliding note.

Rise When the Rooster Crows

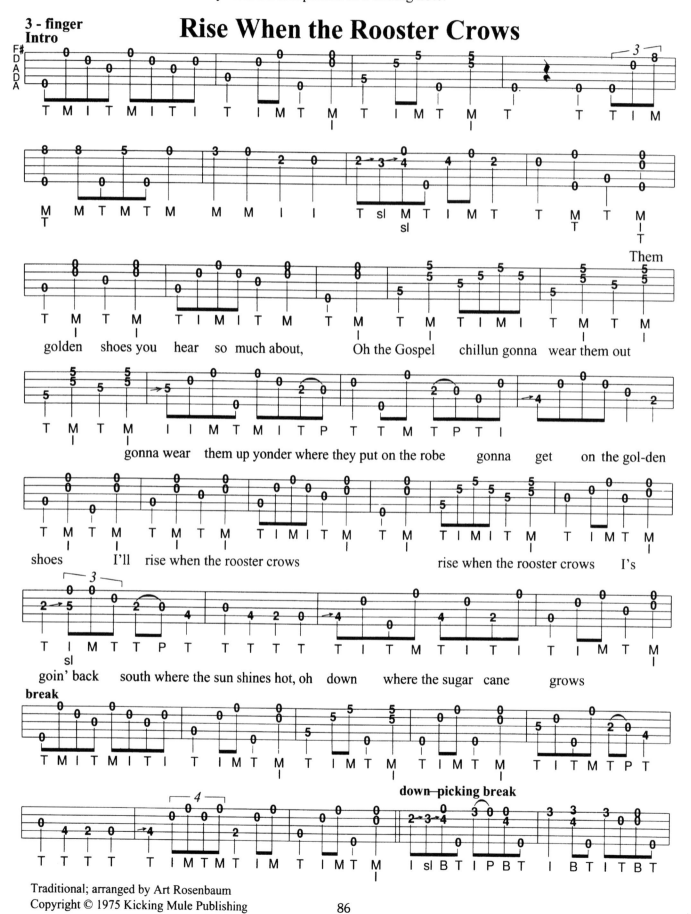

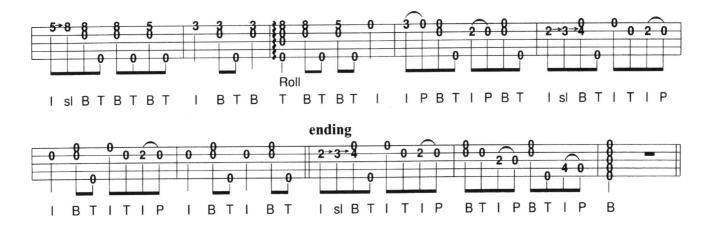

ending

1) Them golden shoes you hear so much about,
   Oh the Gospel Chillun gonna wear them out.
   Gonna wear them up yonder where they put on the robe,
   Gonna put on the golden shoes,

   Chorus: I'll rise when the rooster crows,
                     Rise when the rooster crows,
                     I's goin back south where the sun shines hot,
                     Down where the sugar cane grows.

2) When Gabriel comes for to blow his horn
   No need to pull back for you got to go on,
   Prepare yourself for the great day
   For you can't take money and buy your way,

   Chorus:

3) We'll have cider all the fall,
   And then I'm goin' to the ball
   Where the duck chews tobacco, the goose drinks wine,
   The old hen cackle and the rooster keeps the time.

   Chorus:

   What you gonna do when the women all dead?
   Gonna sit in the corner with a hung-down head.
4) If ever I marry, gonna marry for riches,
   Gonna marry a big fat girl, she can't wear my britches.

   Chorus:

Traditional; arranged by Oren Jenkins
Copyright © 1975 Oren Jenkins

87

Alice Gerrard, Matokie Slaughter, Art Rosenbaum.

SPANISH FANDANGO — DON'T LET YOUR DEAL GO DOWN

Since it was first published in Henry Worrall's *Eclectic Guitar Instructor* over a century ago, the "Spanish Fandango" has surfaced in many forms as a guitar or banjo folk instrumental show piece. This version is taken from Oren Jenkins' playing (Folkways FA2314); Snuffy Jenkins plays it, as well. They learned it from Smith Hammett and Rex Brooks, two influential North Carolina Piedmont 3-finger banjo pickers, who also influenced Earl Scruggs. And Scruggs' role in reintroducing the banjo into country music is a key phenomenon in recent American music. Three finger melodic or accompanying styles were not uncommon in old-time banjo picking, but the relatively smooth transfer of melody lead among thumb, index and middle fingers opened new possibilities for the instrument. "Don't Let Your Deal Go Down" is my proto-bluegrass setting of the great Charlie Poole tune. I play both accompanying and melodic figures around the raggy progression.

TUNING: ᴳDGBD   (Open G tuning)

PICKING: Three – finger.

The SPANISH FANDANGO contains some of the flowing rolls that were subsequently developed into bluegrass banjo. Another proto – bluegrass device occurs in the 10th measure, and elsewhere, where the completion of a slide coincides with a note beginning a reverse roll (MIT). The following chord figures are used:

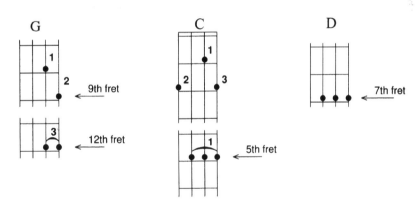

The following chords are used, in this order, in the raggy progression of DON'T
LET YOUR DEAL GO DOWN:

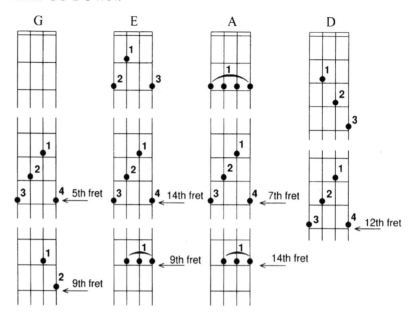

Note that the four - finger chord is convenient movable formation, and is very useful
in playing chord-style three-finger back-up in string band ensembles. With
some practice and a good ear you can work with this and other movable chords in
pieces that call for a chord accompaniment.

Spanish Fandango

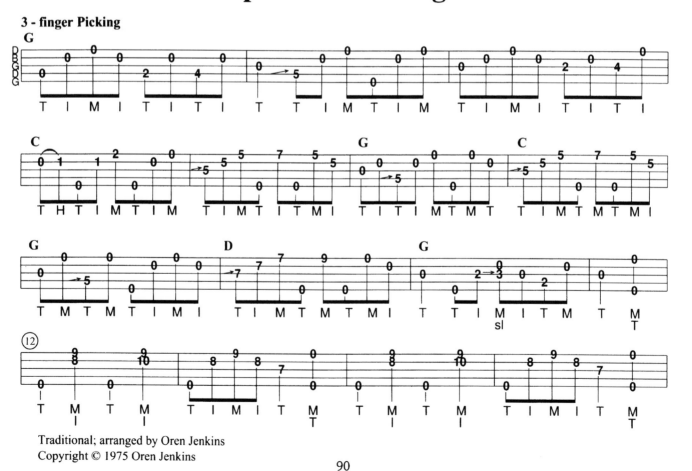

Traditional; arranged by Oren Jenkins
Copyright © 1975 Oren Jenkins

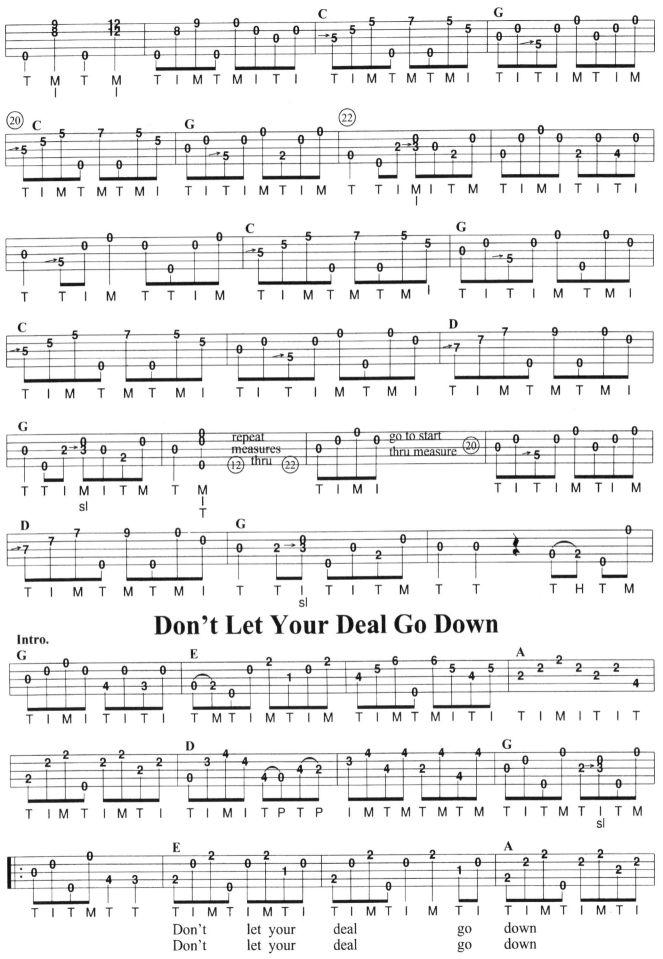

Don't Let Your Deal Go Down

Don't   let your   deal   go   down
Don't   let your   deal   go   down

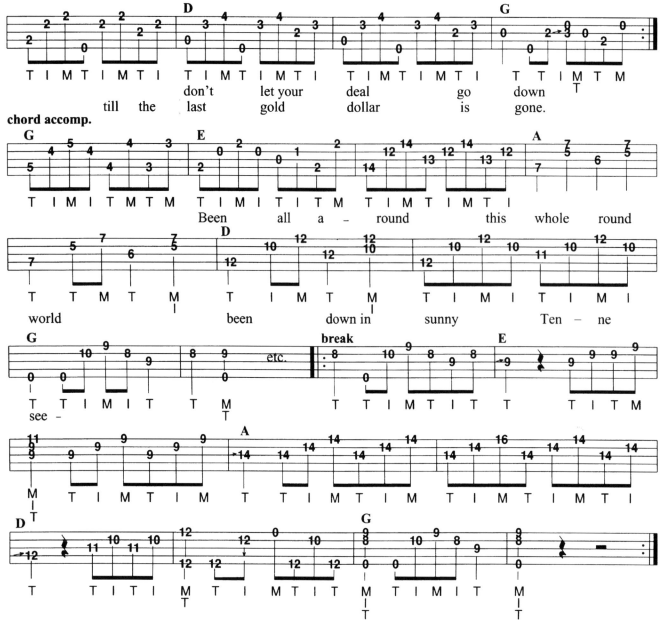

Chorus: Don't let your deal go down,
                Don't let your deal go down.
                Don't let your deal go down
                Till the last gold dollar is gone.

1)   Well you called me a dog when I'm gone,
        Called me a dog when I'm gone,
        When I come round the hill with a twenty dollar bill
        It's "Where have you been so long?"

2)   "Well I been all around this whole round world,
        Been down in sunny Tennessee.
        Any old place I hang my hat
        Is home sweet home to me."

        Chorus

3)   "Where did you get them high-top shoes,
        The dress that you wear so fine?"
        "Got the shoes from a railroad man,
        Dress from a driver in the mine."

        Chorus

92

Buell Kazee, Winchester, KY, 1975 — *Photo: Margo Newmark Rosenbaum*

ABOUT THE AUTHOR

Art Rosenbaum of Athens, Georgia, has been collecting, studying, and performing traditional American music for over 35 years. He sings and plays 5-string banjo, fiddle, guitar and harmonica, and mouth bow. His repertoire, much of it learned first-hand in the course of his field work, ranges from Appalachian banjo tunes and ballads through Southern and Mid-western fiddle tunes to blues and spirituals.

Rosenbaum began seeking out traditional performers while in his teens, rediscovering and recording the great blues guitarist Scrapper Blackwell and recording fiddler John W. Summers, both in his home state of Indiana. He produced LPs of Indiana blues and folk music, the first of the over 1 4 documentary LPs and tapes he has recorded and produced over the years. While living in New York City, he was part of the folk revival of the '50s and '60s, performing as well as organizing concerts of traditional music with the Friends of Old Time Music.

Through the years Rosenbaum has performed in the U.S., Canada, and Europe and appeared at the Newport, Winnipeg, Mariposa, and Philadelphia folk festivals. He has worked solo and in duo with Iowa fiddler Al Murphy and played with string bands such as the Passaic County Chamb'ry Player and Pappy Wells' Ozark Square Dance Band; currently he plays banjo with Phil Tanner's Skillet Lickers of Dacula, Georgia, a continuation of the famous Gid Tanner's Skillet Lickers founded by Phil's grandfather in the 1920s. He has recorded with many folk performers and had two solo recordings on the Kicking Mule label. Among his recent performances are solo concerts in 1995 and 1998 at the Longy School of Music in Cambridge, Massachusetts. He is occasionally joined in performance by Margo Rosenbaum on banjo.

An authority on traditional banjo styles, Rosenbaum wrote two instructional books on the banjo, the influential *Old- Time Mountain Banjo* (Oak Publications, 1968) and *The Art of the Mountain Banjo* (Kicking Mule, 1975). He was a teacher/performer at all three semi-annual sessions of the Tennessee Banjo Institute. He is also author of *Folk Visions and Voices: Traditional Music and Song in North Georgia* (University of Georgia Press, 1983) which also features his drawings and paintings and Margo Newmark Rosenbaum's photographs. Art and Margo Rosenbaum have collaborated on a second book, *Shout Because You're Free: The Ring Shout and its Survival in a Georgia Coastal Community,* released by the University of Georgia Press in 1998. Art Rosenbaum is a regular recording and book reviewer for <u>The Old Time Herald </u>and Art and Margo Rosenbaum were featured in an article in that magazine in 1995. Art was director of the University of Georgia Festival of North Georgia Traditional Music and Dance on the occasion of the 1996 Olympic Games.

Rosenbaum teaches drawing and painting in the Lamar Dodd School of Art, University of Georgia.

Sam McGee

Great Music at Your Fingertips

Made in the USA
Middletown, DE
28 May 2017